TREE OF RENEWED LIFE

TREE OF RENEWED LIFE

Spiritual Renewal of the Church through the Twelve-Step Program

TERRY WEBB

CROSSROAD • NEW YORK

1992

The Crossroad Publishing Company
370 Lexington Avenue, New York, NY 10017

Printed in the United States of America
Typesetting output: TEXSource, Houston

Library of Congress Cataloging-in-Publication Data

Webb, Terry (Mary Theresa)
Tree of renewed life : spiritual renewal of the church through the twelve-step program / Terry Webb.
p. cm.
Includes bibliographical references.
ISBN 0-8245-1140-9 (pbk.)
1. Spiritual life. 2. Twelve-step programs—Religious aspects—Christianity. 3. Church renewal. I. Title.
BV4501.2.W412 1992
269—dc20 91-35754
CIP

Contents

FOREWORD

One of my most indelible memories is that of a totally disreputable figure in a torn undershirt and jeans, held up with a length of clothesline, pushing a wheelbarrow full of seedling trees. Samuel Shoemaker was always happiest planting things . . . trees, gardens, new vision, new ways of thinking about age-old mysteries of God's dealing with humankind.

In this book Terry Webb has used the imagery of the tree to speak of the growth of the "A" groups from their seedling stage to a remarkable movement that has helped tens of thousands to renewed life. In the process the church from which they originally sprang has sometimes learned from, and more often been threatened by, the truths they embody. Perhaps Terry's insightful study will help both rediscover that a spiritual journey is always life-long and that God is a God who likes to surprise us.

In his journal for November 1934 Sam Shoemaker wrote "A significant thing today . . . met Bill Wilson." It surely was . . . for each of them and for the world.

SALLY SHOEMAKER ROBINSON

ACKNOWLEDGMENTS

It was the Holy Spirit, my Higher Power, who first and last inspired and nudged me to complete this work.

My husband and I also owe much to Dave Else, to whom this book is dedicated, who has spent most of his ministry trying to educate clergy and laity that lives do not have to be lost to alcohol and other drugs. He has indeed been a seed planter and a catalyst across the United States, helping addicts and their families.

I acknowledge the support of my husband, who endured a year of my obsessive compulsion with the creation of this book.

Without the encouragement of the First Word, a Christian writers' workshop, I never would have persevered in the task of writing. They read through the first draft of the manuscript and gave me support, editorial comments, and publishing hints. Their prayers undergirded this effort.

Bob Goodley, chair of the Diocesan Alcoholism Commission of the Diocese of New York, provided the first clergy support. Steve Smith, Dave Else, and Brother Tom let me know that it was an important work, as did the National Episcopal Coalition on Alcohol and Drugs. Sally Shoemaker Robinson, now director of Episcopal Social Ministries of the Diocese of Maryland, loaned me some special books of her father's and periodically inquired about my progress. My old friend Betsy Evans taught me about the Oxford Group movement and Frank Buchman. Charles Bishop and John Dowker gave me much-needed historical information about the Washingtonians and Faith at Work. David Baker was my mentor and painstaking editor and critic. He, too, gave me praise and encouragement along the way.

I especially want to thank "Marie" and "Tony" and the other anonymous storytellers who were willing to risk sharing their stories of recovery because they believed in the need for the church to hear.

Thanks to my many friends in recovery who listened to the many bits and pieces of my experience, strength, and hope and who accepted and loved me back to sanity. Thanks to Joe, Don, Marty, Chris, Bill, and Martha, who helped build up my self-esteem enough to be able to tackle this work with confidence.

I want also to acknowledge the assistance Nora Ann gave me in copying the many drafts of the manuscript as well as Bob and the other editors of Crossroads. This book would not be possible without their commitment and dedication.

•

Introduction

THE NEW BEGINNING

> For behold, I will create new heavens and a new earth; the former things will not be remembered, nor will they come to mind. But be glad and rejoice forever in what I will create; for I will create Jerusalem to be a delight and its people a joy.
>
> — Isaiah 65:17, 18, NIV

Creating a new life or a new beginning is what the twelve-step process of recovery from addiction promises. The twelve steps, written by Bill Wilson in 1938 and then adopted by Alcoholics Anonymous, are the basis for the twentieth-century phenomenon known as twelve-step self-help support groups, also known as "A,"[1] or "Anonymous," groups. It is the "A" group process of spiritual renewal about which this book is written.

Only a few churchgoing Christian lay persons and clergy know that these "A" groups were initiated by very devout Christian men, ordained ministers in their denominations. Many think that the self-help groups are completely secular in nature. Little do they realize, because they have not attended meetings themselves, that these groups, meeting in church basements all over the world, may be the hidden church of this century.

Many books have been written about the twelve steps. Two in particular outline in detail the history of the twelve steps, Ernest Kurtz's *Not-God,* and Nan Robertson's *Getting Better.*[2] This book is not an attempt to duplicate these other studies but to recapture and reclaim the roots and the significance of the twelve-step group process of recovery. In a talk at the twentieth anniversary of Alcoholics Anonymous in St. Louis in 1955, Dr. Sam Shoemaker, one of the early leaders of Alcoholics Anonymous, said that AA received its inspiration and impetus indirectly from the insights and beliefs of the church.[3] Father Ed Dowling, another of the founding fathers, compares the twelve-step process to that of Christianity.[4] I believe that the twelve-step movement is a story best described as a mighty work of the Holy Spirit to solve the problem of addiction in this century. I agree with Dr. Shoemaker that God is the moving force that inspires it and keeps it going, which is why the "A" movement is having such a powerful impact.

My intention is to show that the church can be revitalized and reawakened by the insights and practices of Alcoholics Anonymous. Thus, this book has been written for every Christian minister, both lay and ordained, and for devout rabbis and other Jews as well.

This book will also explore the threats to the survival of the twelve-step movement, even at the height of its popularity. Will the twelve-step groups replace the institutional church? Will they survive both the scientific/technological solutions to the disease of addiction and their own trend toward cultism?

My vision for this book is in the form of a tree, a tree whose roots sink deep into a spiritual soil, whose branches are the twelve steps, and whose fruit is every recovering person, beginning with Bill W., Ebby T., and Dr. Bob S. It is a tree whose roots need continually to seek nourishment, thrusting deep into their spiritual soil, a tree that risks withering and dying if it gets cut off from its roots.

I was born and raised in the Anglican tradition and the inspiration for this book came after I attended an Anglican Fellowship of Prayer Conference at Chatham College in Pittsburgh, Pennsylvania, in June 1989. I was in a group discussion with an old friend, Sally Shoemaker Robinson, daughter of the late Rev. Dr. Sam Shoemaker. She brought up the twelve steps in our discussion group. The day after the conference, I created the outline for this book. I have uncovered that Dr. Shoemaker was an inspirational guide for the formation of the twelve steps as well as for the group process known as the fellowship of the "A" groups.

This story is about spiritual renewal and evangelism, a story involving not only my own spiritual rebirth but that of many anonymous individuals, some known only by their first names and some known only by God, who were used by God to give new life to addicts and their families. The renewal movement began in Akron, Ohio, and is now bringing new life even in the Soviet Union. The twelve steps of AA are influencing lives all over the world and bringing people back to a spiritual foundation based, as the twelve steps put it, on surrender to a Higher Power, God "as they understand him," a "Power greater than themselves." This is a silent but powerful revolutionary movement, one of the greatest revival and renewal movements of the twentieth century.

My own rebirth began as my friend Polly and I sat together in an Eat-and-Park on the Ohio River Boulevard in Sewickley, Pennsylvania, while she introduced me to the twelve steps. It was after that introduction in 1981 that I walked into my first "A" meeting. It felt like coming home, and I wondered why I had missed this group all the years of my past life. Polly showed me how to take my personal inventory, and I began the process of working through the twelve steps. I find that "working the steps" is a continual process of allowing God to prune the dead wood from my life. Working through the steps and attending twelve-step meetings has given me gifts of spiritual renewal, discernment, and indescribable experiences of peace and serenity. I have been empowered to a new way of living, a twelve-step kind of living, with each day a new beginning.

Today we are just catching on that addiction is a spiritual as well as a neurological, physiological, and psychological disease.[5] In other words, it is a dis-ease of mind, body, and spirit. In his book *Addiction and Grace*, Dr. Gerald May states that addiction "is the most powerful psychic enemy of humanity's desire for God and makes idolaters of us all, because it forces us to worship these objects of our attachment."[6] Once addiction takes over there is no will power. It is a characteristic of our Western medically and scientifically oriented society to look for medical and scientific solutions to problems, particularly problems of disease. We try to control addiction by legal means, medical research, and psychological gimmicks. We forget that it is a disease that binds the will and destroys the inner life of a person, capturing the soul.

My hope is that both the committed religious and the committed irreligious will "take one thing and leave the rest" from reading this book.

THE TWELVE STEPS

1. We admitted we were powerless over alcohol, that our lives had become unmanageable.
2. Came to believe that a Power greater than ourselves could restore us to sanity.
3. Made a decision to turn our will and our lives over to the care of God as we understood Him.
4. Made a searching and fearless moral inventory of ourselves.
5. Admitted to God, to ourselves and to another human being the exact nature of our wrongs.
6. Were entirely ready to have God remove all these defects of character.
7. Humbly asked Him to remove our shortcomings.
8. Made a list of all persons we had harmed, and became willing to make amends to them all.
9. Made direct amends to such people wherever possible, except when to do so would injure them or others.
10. Continued to take personal inventory and when we were wrong promptly admitted it.
11. Sought through prayer and meditation to improve our conscious contact with God as we understood Him, praying only for knowledge of His will for us and the power to carry that out.
12. Having had a spiritual awakening as the result of these Steps, we tried to carry this message to alcoholics, and to practice these principles in all our affairs.

1

THE ROOTS

Spiritual Beginnings

> In my distress I called to the Lord and he answered me. From the depths of the grave I called for help, and you listened to my cry.
>
> —Jonah 2:2, NIV

"Alcoholics Anonymous is a spiritual program and a spiritual way of life,"[1] and the process of recovery begins when an alcoholic cries out for help or when an addict recognizes that he or she is not God. The twelve steps of Alcoholics Anonymous came as an inspiration of a recovering alcoholic who had a conversion experience in the depth of his despair in the early 1930s. The twelve-step recovery program evolved from the lifelong ministry of this man, Bill Wilson, together with a physician, Dr. Bob Smith; an Episcopal priest, Sam Shoemaker; a Lutheran minister, Frank Buchman; and a Jesuit priest, Father Ed Dowling. The Holy Spirit of God, working through these men, and others, has brought and is bringing new life and light to our addicted world.

Bill Wilson's Conversion

It seemed as if he was at the very bottom of a pit this time at Towns Hospital. Bill Wilson cried out, "If there is a God, let him show himself! I am ready to do anything, anything!"[2] At that moment, a great white light filled the room and he was caught up in an undescribable ecstasy. He suddenly realized that he was free of the bondage of his addiction to alcohol and a wonderful sense of God's presence surrounded him.[3] He had been in Towns Hospital many times before, under the care of Dr. William D. Silkworth. Dr. Silkworth had tried to explain to him that he had an addict's disease, an allergy to alcohol, which had taken over his life, causing him blackouts and all kinds of problems. But Bill Wilson was stubborn. He had kept promising to stop drinking. Each time he sobered up he had gone back to drinking, and each time his disease became a little worse.

Earlier that year, Bill Wilson, a New York stockbroker, had found himself at the Calvary Mission in the Skid Row district of New York City. The mission was founded by Episcopal priest Sam Shoemaker, who was later to become a close friend of Bill's and spiritual guide for the formation of the twelve steps.

Bill had been bar-hopping that night. He met his friend Ebby at the mission and ate some beans before heading out to church for an evening of gospel and hymn singing. There he responded to an altar call and committed his life to Christ.[4] He barely had a chance to consider what that response meant when he started drinking again. He needed to land in Towns Hospital one more time to have his body cleansed of alcohol before he could admit the truth of his helplessness and powerlessness over his disease.

These spiritual experiences began to transform Bill Wilson. When he was discharged from the hospital, he started attending Oxford Group meetings and working at the Calvary Mission, zealously trying to save other alcoholics like himself. These spiritual conversion experiences gave Bill the underpinnings for his sobriety, but it was his regular attendance at Oxford Group meetings with friend Ebby in New York and then Dr. Bob in Akron that gave him the long-term support to maintain his sobriety.

A Lutheran Minister and a First-Century Christian Fellowship

Ebby T. was Bill's life-long friend and drinking buddy. In fact Bill calls him his sponsor.[5] It was Ebby who first talked to Bill about a "religious" way to stay sober. Bill tells the story as follows:

> The door opened and he stood there, fresh-skinned and glowing. There was something about his eye. He was inexplicably different. What had happened? I pushed a drink across the table. He refused it. Disappointed but curious, I wondered what had got into the fellow. He wasn't himself.

> "Come, what's all this about?" I queried. He looked straight at me. Simply, but smilingly, he said, "I've got religion." I was aghast. So that was it — last summer an alcoholic crackpot; now, I suspected, a little cracked about religion. He had that starry-eyed look. Yes, the old boy was on fire all right. But bless his heart, let him rant! Besides, my gin would last longer than his preaching.[6]

Ebby had found his "salvation" from his drinking at an Oxford Group meeting he had been dragged to by friend Rowland H. After his conversion experiences, Bill W. also began to associate himself with the Oxford Group movement. Ebby eventually died of his alcoholism, while Bill was to remain sober until his death.

The Oxford Group movement, organized along the lines of first-century models of Christian fellowship, was founded by Frank Buchman, a Lutheran minister and a native of Allentown, Pennsylvania. His conversion came about after he had heard a Salvation Army sermon in England in 1908. On fire with zeal for the Lord, he called himself "a soul surgeon."[7] First he became secretary of the Young Men's Christian Association at Pennsylvania State College and then, in 1918, went to China as a missionary. There he evangelized others through small group Christian fellowship and discipling. His evangelistic zeal led him back to England, where the Oxford Group movement received its name. He met Sam Shoemaker in China, the two of them became good friends, and he influenced Sam to go into ordained ministry. Later, Sam was to become the leader of the Oxford Group movement in the United States.

The two co-founders of Alcoholics Anonymous, Dr. Bob and Bill W., with their friend Ebby T., owed much of their early impetus for sobriety to their attendance at the Oxford small group meetings, called "house parties" because they met in each other's homes. Dr. Bob first shared the secret of his drinking at an Oxford Group meeting in Akron, Ohio. Bill W. did the same after his conversion experiences in 1934. All three men turned to the Bible for solace, paying particular attention to the Sermon on the Mount and the Epistle of James.[8] They stayed with the Oxford Group movement until AA was founded. Alcoholics Anonymous says that it was the Oxford Group movement that paved the way for Alcoholics Anonymous. The movement showed them what to do and what not to do.[9]

About the time that the Oxford Group movement became known as Moral Re-Armament, in 1938, both Sam Shoemaker and Bill W. became discouraged with the movement.[10] By then it was at the height of its popularity, an alternative to arming for war. Big public rallies and media campaigns were in vogue. But the tempo, glamor, and popularity were not good for the egos of recovering alcoholics. Sam Shoemaker's break came when he discerned that Frank Buchman, with his dominating, charismatic personality, was becoming more authoritarian and increasingly critical of the institutional church. Sam returned to full-time service in the Episcopal Church and Bill W. turned to full-time service with Alcoholics Anonymous. Later Sam commented to his friends in AA that he hoped they would not forget the roots of the program in the "primitive" fundamentalist kind of Christianity that the Oxford Group movement exemplified.[11]

An Anglican Priest: A Spiritual Giant

Sam Shoemaker and his wife, Helen, have had a tremendous impact on the life of the church in the twentieth century. Sam was ordained deacon in the Episcopal Church in 1920 and a priest in 1921. He spent twenty-five years as rector of Calvary Church in New York and then accepted a call to Calvary Church in Pittsburgh. While in New York he helped found Alcoholics Anonymous, as well as Faith at Work, a small group fellowship. Sam was an evangelist, a dynamic preacher, and a leader. He believed his main purpose in life was to bring people to Christ.

Sam Shoemaker and Bill Wilson were long-time friends. Sam was Bill Wilson's spiritual guide and mentor, and Bill said that it was through Sam that most of AA's spiritual principles came. "How well I remember that first day I caught sight of him," Bill recalled. "It was a Sunday service in his church. I can see him standing before the lectern. His utter honesty, his tremendous forthrightness, struck me deep. I shall never forget it."[12]

Sam Shoemaker was one of the forgotten founders of AA. His tenets regarding faith, conversion, honesty with oneself, self-examination, character defects, prayer, getting in touch with God's Power, fellowship, being in a company of sinners, witness, and working with others were incorporated into the program. Sam was there when AA needed synthesis, and he offered positive spiritual input. Sam called AA "one of the great signs of spiritual awakening of our time." He claimed that his association with AA was one of the most joyous things in his life.[13]

As rector of Calvary Episcopal Church in New York City, Sam founded Calvary Mission in 1926. For many days he had walked by an unused chapel in the seedy Gas Light district and mused about how "a vital church should be reaching . . . to those without place in society, the homeless, friendless, faithless derelicts who have lost everything."[14] He appointed Henry Hadley as the first director of the mission, and Henry would read Bible verses to the men who drifted in to listen to gospel hymns. Calvary Mission became the model for other missions around the country.

A Jesuit Priest

Rev. Ed Dowling, a Jesuit priest, was a positive influence on AA and helped win its acceptance in the Roman Catholic Church. As a result of his recommendation the Alcoholics Anonymous "Big Book" was approved by the New York archdiocese in 1939. Previously, the Roman Catholic Church would have little to do with AA because of its involvement with the Oxford Group movement. In 1940, Father Ed started the first AA group in St. Louis. Father Ed saw much similarity between the Spiritual Exercises of St. Ignatius and the twelve steps.[15]

Bill Wilson describes his first encounter with Father Ed:

> I heard labored footsteps on the stairs. Then, balanced precariously on his cane, he came into the room, carrying a battered black hat that was shapeless as a cabbage leaf and plastered with sleet. He lowered himself into my solitary chair, and when he opened his overcoat I saw his clerical collar. He brushed back a shock of white hair and looked at me through the most remarkable pair of eyes I have ever seen. We talked about a lot of things, and my spirits kept on rising, and presently I began to realize that this man radiated a grace that filled the room with a sense of presence. I felt this with great intensity; it was a moving and mysterious experience. In years since I have seen much of this great friend, and whether I was in joy or in pain he always brought to me the same sense of grace and the presence of God.[16]

Like Sam Shoemaker, Father Ed saw a spark of the divine in men suffering from alcoholism. It was through their patience, their acceptance, their willingness to be involved and to be available that alcoholics began to experience life again. Even when Bill W., in a drunken spree, threw a rock through a window in Calvary Church, he was still welcomed.

The Prayers

> Real prayer is not telling God what we want. It is putting ourselves at His disposal so that He can tell us what He wants.
>
> — Sam Shoemaker

There are three prayers that have had great impact on the life of Alcoholics Anonymous and other Anonymous self-help groups: the Lord's Prayer, the prayer attributed to St. Francis of Assisi, and the Serenity Prayer. These prayers are among the spiritual roots of the renewed tree of life for recovering addicts and their families. The two most frequently said prayers in the early days of AA were the Lord's Prayer and the St. Francis Prayer. Not only did the founders of Alcoholics Anonymous use these prayers at the beginning and end of their meetings but they included Bible studies as well. Today most meetings use only the Serenity Prayer and the Lord's Prayer.

The St. Francis Prayer

Lord, make us instruments of your peace.
Where there is hatred, let us sow love;
where there is injury, pardon;
where there is discord, union;
where there is doubt, faith;
where there is despair, hope;
where there is darkness, light;
where there is sadness, joy.
Grant that we may not so much seek
to be consoled as to console;
to be understood as to understand;
to be loved as to love.
For it is in giving that we receive;
it is in pardoning that we are pardoned;
and it is in dying that we are born to eternal life.

— attributed to St. Francis

Although the St. Francis Prayer is not frequently used today in AA, it is used in Al-Anon, the "A" groups for families of alcoholics, and it is printed on "Just For Today" cards.[17]

St. Francis, a famous monk, peacemaker, and healer of the Middle Ages, found that he could not be a true follower of Christ until he could embrace a leper. Alcoholics, like lepers, even today are stigmatized and made outcasts of society, often by well-meaning Christians. This prayer, attributed to St. Francis, was a favorite of Bill Wilson's. It is a prayer of hope and of new life. Much like the psalms, it encapsulates life, which is at one moment full of pain, hatred, rejection, and conflict and, at another, because of God's intercession, full of peace, love, and joy.

The Lord's Prayer

Our Father who art in heaven,
Hallowed be thy name.
Thy kingdom come,
thy will be done,
on earth as it is in heaven.
Give us this day our daily bread;
and forgive us our trespasses,
as we forgive those who trespass against us;
and lead us not into temptation,
but deliver us from evil.
For thine is the kingdom, the power and the glory for ever.
Amen.

— Matthew 6:9–13[18]

It is 9:30 p.m. They gather in the undercrofts and basements of churches and in meeting rooms in cities and towns throughout the U.S.A. They've listened and shared their experiences, strengths, and hopes. At these AA meetings there are usually more than fifty people gathered, men and women, young and old, black and white, Jews and Christians and non-believers. They rise from their chairs as the chairperson for the evening says, "Would all who care to join me in the 'Our Father' "? All join hands and bow their heads and say the familiar Lord's Prayer.

Some Jews feel uneasy about AA and, specifically, about reciting the Lord's Prayer, which they consider to be Christian. Yet it was a Jewish rabbi named Jesus, or Yeshua (which means "savior" in Hebrew), who first taught this prayer. The prayer outlines for us what our attitude should be about God and about the lives we lead. It also summarizes the twelve-step way of life, expressing dependence on a personal God, through surrender to a Higher Power. Its petitions are similar to the benedictions in the Jewish *Amida*[19] and to the twelve steps. Those who pray the Lord's Prayer make a commitment to follow that Higher Power.

As people followed Jesus around Galilee, they often saw him go off by himself into the hills to pray. Like all devout Jews, he prayed privately three times a day. Jesus' followers had seen the Pharisees pray in public, with much bowing and lamentation. But Jesus' technique of praying was not like that of the Pharisees. His attitude was one of deep devotion and reverence rather than outward show. The people had seen Jesus go regularly to the synagogue worship service on the Sabbath. They too were used to practicing daily prayers. But when Jesus prayed it was different. Even when he read the scriptures he did so with authority and conviction.

One day his followers saw Jesus at prayer, and one asked him to teach them how to pray, just as John the Baptist had taught his followers. The prayer that he taught them can be described as follows:

"Abba Father." For Jesus' Jewish followers this was an unfamiliar way of addressing God. In their synagogues today, Jews address God as *Avenu,* Our Father, Our King, Our Redeemer. They are petitioners coming before a Majestic Presence. But "Abba Father" was and is today a too familiar way of addressing God. It is like calling God "Daddy." "Yahweh" or "Adoni" were more respectful terms. Even Isaiah spoke God's name with great awe and reverence. God was too holy to be addressed with such familiarity. Jesus' hearers were taught to honor their own fathers, who were the heads of the family. As children, they looked to their fathers for food and guidance.[20] Jesus was saying that the holy, revered God of their ancestors was like a nurturing parent. "Because you are sons, God sent forth the spirit of his Son into your hearts, crying Abba Father!" (Gal. 4:6). Jesus taught his followers that they must depend on God, not on themselves or each other. This new teaching got their attention.

"Who art in heaven." God was in his usual place in heaven, separate and apart from human beings, but overseeing all that they did. When God is in heaven, all should be right with the world. *"Hallowed be your name."* Pious Jews were used to honoring God. God's name was the HOLY ONE, or YAHWEH. The Jewish followers of Jesus were not used to saying God's name. God's name was power and authority and was too awesome to say aloud. God didn't need any witnesses to the truth of who he was. He was the great "I am." Surrender everything to this Heavenly

God, said Jesus, including your life. Rabbi Moshe Chaim Luzzatto, writing in the 1700s, stated that "there is only one true good . . . and that is attachment to God."[21] In the fourth century, Augustine of Hippo, one of the fathers of Western Christianity, wrote that our hearts are restless until they rest in God. In the nineteenth century, Frances Ridley Havergal wrote these words in a hymn, "Take my life and let it be, consecrated Lord to thee."[22] Seeking this attachment to a Higher Power, human beings can then make the petitions that follow.

"Thy kingdom come." This was the first petition. Jesus' followers had long anticipated the coming of the Messiah, their long-awaited king, like David, who would establish his kingdom and do away with the Romans. Once again their land would belong to them and the government would be theirs, not controlled by a foreign nation. Hadn't Isaiah prophesied that this would happen? Jesus' followers anticipated this glorious kingdom when God's Shalom would be all-encompassing, when the lion would lie down with the lamb, and the world would know eternal peace. How they longed for that day!

"Thy will be done, on earth as it is in heaven." In the second petition Jesus taught that it must be God's will, not ours, that we pray for. Jesus' followers had heard many times of the people's continual rebellion against God during their forty years in the wilderness. They knew the prophets' admonitions. They just couldn't see the signs in their own day. Every time disaster struck, whenever there was a famine, a plague, or an earthquake, or a foreign nation took them into exile and occupied their land, they had to repent and turn to God to receive his bountiful mercy once again.

Jesus knew that we are too prone to want to do it our own way and want instant results. It is only in recognizing our powerlessness, our helplessness that we can cooperate with God. It is only by recognizing the priority of God in our lives and surrendering ourselves that we can receive God's mercy and forgiveness. We must die to our self-will and be obedient to God's will, however long it takes, however reluctant we are. It is a daily process and requires a willingness to face our willfulness, our rebellion, our stubbornness, and to turn all this imperfection over to God peacefully, joyfully, and in a disciplined way.

God wasn't simply some distant heavenly being that Jesus' followers could spiritualize away to heaven. Jesus taught that God was concerned about earthly matters, that history was *his* story, that God would give the people free reign — up to a point. When people began to turn away from doing God's will and doing "their own thing," God would see to it that they recognized that He was in charge.

"Give us this day our daily bread." This was the third petition. Jesus taught his followers over and over again that God would provide for them. Hadn't God given them *manna* in the wilderness for forty years? Manna was an edible gum, sweet droppings from the tamarisk tree that formed iridescent balls, which the people gathered early in the morning and made into cakes. It was like a gift from heaven, which could be ground, baked, or broiled, but could be kept for only a day. It provided just enough for their daily needs.[23] God wanted his people to depend on him to meet their daily needs. God would provide one day at a time. But the people were greedy and wanted more manna and more variety in their daily diet. They hoarded what they had and worried about the future. In spite of their rebelliousness, God had led them to a land of "milk and honey," a land of brooks and water, which produced wheat and barley and long-lasting fig and olive trees. The Jews who followed Jesus were used to *artos*, a kind of barley bread, mixed with beans or lentils. It was just plain bread for plain people. Nothing fancy, it was round with a hole in the middle. It was baked fresh daily in large ovens or kilns and was sufficient for that day. At the beginning of every Jewish meal it was offered to God by the father of the household. Jesus put the emphasis on "daily," enough sustenance to keep one going for today and the immediate future. The people could depend on God to meet their daily needs because he loved them.

"And forgive us our trespasses, as we forgive those who trespass against us." The fourth petition is about forgiveness. All Jesus' followers were familiar with the sin offerings in the temple. But doves or grain were about all they could afford to offer. If you became unclean by touching a dead body, through disease, or by breaking the law, atonement could be made through these sacrifices at the temple. Forgiveness for devout Jews to this day is proactive rather than passive. Human beings have an obligation to reach out, to seek forgiveness from those offended. Jews believe that to be at enmity with each other is to be at enmity with God. There is a Jewish prayer of forgiveness that can be said on the eve of Rosh Hashanah:[24]

> Our God and God of our Fathers, let our prayer reach you — do not turn away from our pleading. For we are not so arrogant and obstinate to claim that we are indeed righteous people and have

never sinned. But we know that both we and our fathers have sinned.

We have abused and betrayed. We are cruel.

We have destroyed and embittered other people's lives.

We were false to ourselves.

We gave gossiped about others and hated them.

We have insulted and jeered. We have killed.

We have lied.

We have misled others and neglected them.

We were obstinate. We have perverted and quarrelled.

We have robbed and stolen.

We have transgressed through unkindness.

We have been both violent and weak.

We have practiced extortion.

We have yielded to wrong desires, our zeal was misplaced.

We turn away Your commandments and good judgement but it does not help us.

Your justice exists whatever happens to us, for evil.

What can we tell you — Your being is remote as the heavens? Yet you know everything, hidden and revealed.

You know the mysteries of the universe and the intimate secrets of everyone alive. You probe our body's state.

You see into the heart and mind. Nothing escapes You, nothing is hidden from Your gaze. Our God and God of our fathers, have mercy on us and pardon all our sins; grant atonement for all our iniquities, forgiveness for all our transgressions.

— A Jewish Prayer of Atonement[25]

Jesus too taught that forgiveness, for others as well as for ourselves, is an ongoing process. It is essential to a right relationship with a Holy God, to being part of God's reign. Forgiveness is also essential to the recovery process from addiction. As we offer our broken spirit to God, through the twelve steps, God reaches down to touch us. First we must recognize the guilt and be willing to make amends. Penance, beginning with a list of all the persons we have harmed, is the next step and is essential to letting go of the guilt and receiving the free gift of God's forgiveness. God doesn't keep old score cards; God doesn't hold grudges and neither must we. But it is a stern and painful process, this searching of the soul, and requires a willingness to right what is wrong in ourselves.

Through Christ, God's forgiveness for us is proactive. Therefore, the saints, said St. Teresa, "rejoiced at injuries and persecutions [by others], because in forgiving them they had something to offer God."[26] Like Ornan's offering to God of his threshing floor (1 Chron. 21), like the offering of our goods and our money, our offering of forgiveness to others for the wrongs done to us is our response to God for his everlasting mercy to us.

"Lead us not into temptation, but deliver us from evil." This last petition was a plea for protection. Jesus knew too well that his followers would be tempted to fall away from God. He even told Peter that he would deny him three times. We live in a spiritual world, and Satan is there to be the tempter, sometimes in the most subtle ways. Jesus went through his own time of temptation during his forty-day fast in the wilderness before he began his ministry. But God is not a source of temptation and does not allow us to be tempted beyond our ability to endure:

> For God cannot be tempted by evil, and he himself tempts no one. But a person is tempted when he is drawn away and trapped by his own evil desire. Then his evil desire conceives and gives birth to sin, and sin when it is full-grown, gives birth to death.
>
> (James 1:14–15 GNB)

Jesus' Jewish followers knew that "the Lord watches over the righteous and listens to their prayers; but he opposes those who do evil" (Ps. 34:15–16). He taught them that no one could enter God's reign without going through a period of temptation and keeping the faith.

For addicts, resisting the temptation to use again requires being able to recognize the symptoms of relapse and the subtle "urges" or triggers to use. Working the AA program is cooperating with God. "Hitting your knees" on a daily basis and asking for God's protection to get through that day without being tempted to use is important to recovery.

"For thine is the kingdom, the Power and the Glory." Prayer ends, Jesus taught, with the recognition of the transcendence of God. "Glory," said the rabbis, "that brightness on the face of man, in which the created order gave back a faint reflection of the Eternal Radiance, was the first thing lost by Adam in the Fall."[27] Jesus' Jewish followers could not look into the face of God, so often they had fallen away from God.

But God, that Power greater than ourselves, can and does restore brokenness to wholeness, dis-ease to ease, insanity to saneness, willfulness to willingness, rebellion to surrender — so that we can sing these familiar words from the Sanctus:

> Holy, Holy, Holy, Lord God of Hosts,
> Heaven and earth are full of thy Glory.
> Glory be to thee, O Lord most high.
> Blessed is he who cometh in the name of the Lord.
> Hosanna in the highest. Amen.

The Lord's Prayer is fully a Jewish prayer adopted by the People of the Way. Today Jewish scholars recognize that all elements of the Our Father can be found in Jewish traditional teaching on prayer. But Jesus put all the elements together in a new way.

The first followers of Jesus kept to the Jewish religious traditions and customs. They attended synagogue regularly and prayed the way Jesus taught them to pray. It wasn't much different from what they had been used to. Yet, they knew God now in an intimate way and they were empowered to a new way of living. The Our Father became a part of their tradition. Their brokenness could now be made whole through Jesus Christ whereas before they had to rely on following the Torah to be holy. Jesus Christ would be alive yesterday, today, and always, through his Holy Spirit, for all people everywhere. Like Moses in the wilderness of sin, like Isaiah the prophet, now all people everywhere could know his glory, the glory of the Only Begotten Son, full of grace and truth!

As the followers of Jesus grew in number, they were persecuted by their compatriots and then by the Romans so that they had to meet secretly in each other's homes. They had to work on their own forgiveness in the midst of the persecutions and the injustices they encountered. The prayer that Jesus had taught them became very special, because of their deep and abiding love for him. It has been a special prayer for persons today in all walks of life and for all religious persuasions. It was intended originally for the Jewish followers of Yeshua, the Savior, born of the house and lineage of David, of royalty. It is this living Jesus who still today is in the midst of his people and works through the twelve-step process to heal broken and hopeless addicts and their family members.

The Serenity Prayer

> God, give us the serenity to accept what cannot be changed;
> give us the courage to change what should be changed;
> give us the wisdom to distinguish one from the other.
>
> — credited to Reinhold Niebuhr

It was a summer day in Heath, Massachusetts, in the late 1930s. The summer residents had gathered for the regular Sunday worship service at the Heath Evangelical United Church. The preacher for the summer months was Dr. Reinhold Niebuhr, noted not only for his brilliant and earthy exegesis of scripture, which was full of grace and truth, but also for his pragmatic relativism and neo-orthodoxy.[28] His congregation anticipated an evangelical sermon as well as practical wisdom to apply to daily living in those prewar years.[29]

Before he began the service that Sunday, according to Dr. Niebuhr, he casually jotted down what has come to be known as the Serenity Prayer. It was adopted by AA in 1939, with the wording slightly changed:

> God grant me the serenity to accept the things I cannot change,
> Courage to change the things I can,
> And wisdom to know the difference.

In Everywhere, U.S.A., Moscow, U.S.S.R., and other places around the world, recovering addicts and their families say this prayer at the beginning or end of their twelve-step meetings. It was quoted and attributed to Kurt Vonnegut, Jr., by Sergei M. Plekhanov, one of the leaders of the two houses of government in the Soviet Union,[30] and by President Bush at the end of the Malta summit meeting with Gorbachev.[31]

Reinhold Niebuhr is credited with authorship of the Serenity Prayer by both AA and several edited collections of prayers.[32] He is also credited with authorship of a much longer prayer:

> God grant me the serenity to accept the things I cannot change;
> Courage to change the things I can,
> and Wisdom to know the difference.
> Living one day at a time;
> Enjoying one moment at a time;
> Accepting hardship as the Pathway to peace;

Taking, as He did, this sinful world as it is,
not as I would have it;
Trusting that He will make all things right,
if I surrender to His will;
That I may be reasonably happy in this life,
and supremely happy with Him forever in the next. Amen.[33]

Misty J. Thigpen describes the confusion surrounding Niebuhr's authorship of the Serenity Prayer in an article entitled, "The Not-So-Serene Origins of the Serenity Prayer."[34] Seith Kastern, Union Theological Seminary librarian in charge of the archives, refutes any claim that Dr. Niebuhr wrote the longer version of the Serenity Prayer attributed to him.[35] The Anglican publishing house Mobray of London identifies the Serenity Prayer as a general or common prayer of fourteenth-century England.[36] Bill Wilson, the founder of AA, believed that "no one can tell for sure who first wrote the Serenity Prayer."[37] Perhaps it came from the early Greeks, perhaps from an anonymous English poet, perhaps from an American naval officer, perhaps from a German dean of Weinsberg.[38] The prayer used to introduce a sermon at a Sunday worship service in Heath was probably deeply embedded in the subconscious of a man of great faith, a prayer that he could have heard in German at one time in his life. In any case, when he first saw the prayer in print, Bill W. declared that "never had we seen so much AA in so few words."[39]

Current research shows that pinpointing authorship of the Serenity Prayer is impossible. We can only take educated guesses. The more facts we have, the more confusing the picture becomes. And does it really matter? For it seems that the prayer has reappeared throughout the centuries, in one form or another, whenever it gave meaning to life or made us aware of our own powerlessness and need for the Holy, Transcendent, Immanent Spirit of God. The prayer is the work of that Spirit, among men and women of faith. Reinhold Niebuhr, like Sam Shoemaker and Frank Buchman, was a man of prayer who was attuned to the Holy Spirit.

According to Dr. Niebuhr, after he used the prayer in his sermon at the Evangelical Heath United Church that summer, Dr. Howard Chandler Robbins, chairman of the workshop committee of the World Council of Churches, called him to ask if he could use the prayer in his monthly report.[40] The prayer was later printed on cards for soldiers during World War II and became the official motto of the West German Army Academy after the war. Alcoholics Anonymous claims that Bill W.'s friend Howard saw the prayer in an obituary in the *New York Herald Tribune* in June 1940. He liked it so much he had it printed on cards and incorporated it into the AA literature.[41]

Dr. Niebuhr often lamented that the prayer became known as the Serenity Prayer, for he was an ethicist and social critic and considered a prophet to politicians. He did not intend that this prayer would be used to avoid dealing with injustice and conflict. Quite the contrary; his theology was one of social praxis. It was a theology of hope, a hope that came through creative and transformative political and social action for justice, equality, and peace.[42]

For the recovering alcoholic or addict, the Serenity Prayer, said over and over again, leads to a renewed faith and hope in a God who acts to bring health and help in the midst of despair. Bill Wilson phrased it this way:

> In the radiance of this prayer we see that defeat, rightly accepted, need be no disaster. We now know that we do not have to run away, nor ought we again try to overcome adversity by still another bulldozing power drive that can only push up obstacles before us faster than they can be taken down.[43]

A family member in recovery in Al-Anon commented:

> Saying the Serenity Prayer has always given me both a Peace of Mind and hope that God is in control and will make all things right in His time. It keeps me from wallowing in self-pity and destructive negative thinking. Just when I want to give up, God provides a new door open and a new path to try. He gives me the courage, the insight and the wisdom that I ask for. So I keep on speaking. I keep on trying to change the things I can.

The Serenity Prayer is an admission of our dependence on a Holy God and an acceptance of our powerlessness and unmanageability. It epitomizes a peace of mind and a quietness of the soul that comes from acceptance and surrender. Without God, we are hopeless and helpless and prone to go our own way, which leads to destruction. Peace and serenity come only when we can accept our human condition and turn our human frailties and shortcomings over to God.

The prayer asks God to provide what we cannot provide for ourselves, the courage to change, to allow God to change us and to make us his instruments for change in society. It asks God to help us move away from our obsessions and addictions.

Finally the Serenity Prayer asks God to give us the wisdom to know when to act and to know when it is best to step back and wait. It helps us to recognize new doors that will open when there seems no way out, new opportunities in the face of defeat. It helps us wait for God's timing. "Let go and let God" is a simple paraphrase of what the prayer is all about.[44]

2

THE TRUNK

Small Group Fellowship

There is an old rabbinic tale: The Lord said to the Rabbi, "Come, I will show you hell." They entered a room where a group of people sat around a huge pot of stew. Everyone was famished and desperate. Each held a spoon that reached the pot but had a handle so long it could not be used to reach their mouths. The suffering was terrible.

"Come, now I will show you heaven," the Lord said after a while. They entered another room, identical to the first — the pot of stew, the group of people, the same long spoons. But there everyone was happy and nourished. "I don't understand," said the Rabbi. "Why are they happy here when they were miserable in the other room, and everything was the same?" The Lord smiled. "Ah, but don't you see?" He said, "Here they have learned to feed each other."

— from *Hearts That We Broke Long Ago,* by Merle Shain

The Washingtonians

When the first Pilgrims settled at Plymouth Rock they brought with them kegs of rum and sat around in British-style taverns drinking beer and ale. By 1744 Ben Franklin was decrying drunkenness before the grand jury of Philadelphia. In 1784 Dr. Benjamin Rush, a signer of the Declaration of Independence, identified chronic drunkenness as a disease, and alcohol, which these early Americans considered safer than water to drink, as an addictive drug. His identification of alcoholism as a disease coincided with the beginning of the temperance movement in America. It was the temperance movement that spawned the first small support group for alcoholics called the Washingtonians. It began with six drunks in Baltimore in 1840. They decided to attend a temperance meeting and to try to stay sober by helping each other and taking a pledge to stay abstinent from "King Alcohol." An example of one pledge that the Juvenile Washington Temperance Benevolent Society adopted was:

A pledge to make,
No wine to take,
Nor Brandy, red,
To turn the head,
Nor whiskey hot,
That makes the sot,
Nor fiery rum,
That ruins the home,
Nor will we sin,
by drinking gin,
Hard cider, too,
Will never do,
Nor brewer's beer,
Our hearts to cheer,
To quench our thirst,
We always bring cold water,
From the well or spring.
So here we pledge perpetual hate,
To all that can intoxicate.[1]

They were supported financially by the temperance activists in the churches. They gave speeches all up and down the East coast. Within ten years there were one hundred and fifty thousand drunks meeting to try and keep each other sober. Abraham Lincoln said of the Washingtonians, "Those whom they desire to convince and persuade are their old friends and companions. They know they are not demons nor even the worst of men."[2]

Then as now, drunkenness was considered a moral issue, a matter of a lack of will power. But after a phenomenal growth period these early communities of recovering drunks died out. Some started drinking again and left the groups. In many groups there was dissension within their ranks from the very temperance prohibitionists that had helped them from the beginning. Some clergy also opposed them.

The Boiler Room Gang

In the 1930s the concept of drunks helping drunks to stay sober caught on again, inspired by two clergymen who tried to revitalize the institutional church through weekly small group fellowship meetings where ordinary people could gather to share their faith.

The first "A" group was modeled after the experience of those who found that regular sharing times were important in Christian living. One such group began in a boiler room of a church basement in New York City. Herbie, the janitor, and Bill Levine, a Jewish painter, first met when Bill came to do some painting of the Calvary Church parish hall in 1940.[3] One day Herbie began to share his experience of being a Christian with Bill in the boiler room of the church. Soon they were meeting frequently there, studying the Bible together and praying, until eventually Bill became a Christian. Then Ralston Young, a redcap porter, joined them. Ralston decided to start similar small group sharing meetings with travelers at Grand Central Station. There, seated around the benches waiting between trains, travelers shared experiences, strengths and hopes. Ralston Young carried not only baggage but people's burdens as well.[4] Eventually the groups got so large they acquired their own building and changed their name to Faith at Work. The organization still draws people from all walks of life, meeting weekly to teach and advance the Christian faith.

In the same Calvary Church building, on Tuesday nights, meetings of Alcoholics Anonymous were held. The principles of AA — acceptance, sharing, caring, and modeling — paralleled those of the Boiler Room Gang. Sam Shoemaker said that the basic approach used by the Boiler Room Gang could be used by anyone with problems, "for everyone has a problem, is a problem, or lives with a problem."[5] Dr. Shoemaker believed in small groups for evangelism, where people could be drawn together by a common need. One person sharing a story is like the leaven in bread, the catalyst that makes the bread live. Dr. Shoemaker's enthusiastic support of this type of meeting later led to the Pittsburgh Experiment, which began when he gathered some of that city's leading industrialists and socialites at a country club to share their faith. Some of the great lay leadership in the Episcopal church came out of these two discipling groups, Faith Alive and the Pittsburgh Experiment. Sam's encouragement for the same group process for recovering alcoholics was critical in the early days of AA.

Oxford Group Movement

The Oxford Group movement began when several students and their professors met together at Oxford College to support one another in disciplined Christian living. The Oxford Group, or clubs, as they were called, provided an alternative way of life, one with structure and uncompromising standards of honesty, purity, unselfishness, and love. The group provided an alternative to the lax Christian living of those around them. Many who were drawn to the group were agnostics who had read the Bible but were cynical because they had never seen Christianity really lived.

Between 1931 and 1935, about 150 undergraduates met daily to fully commit their lives to God.[6] This was an intense kind of spiritual training whose purpose was to build a new world and an alternative to the Communist cell groups that were proliferating at the time. The Oxford Group movement became a fellowship of travelers who followed a pilgrim's way. It gave its followers new hearts and courage and hope. It was essentially an intellectual, middle-class movement and spread rapidly to the United States and Canada.[7] In the United States, members met in each other's homes and the meetings became known as "house parties." They were very similar to Quaker meetings or Cursillo reunion group meetings.[8] The Bible was read, prayers and personal testimony were shared. A sense of closeness to God and to each other prevailed and one could sense God's presence in the quiet times.

At first, the Oxford Group meetings were interdenominational. Anyone could belong, and members were encouraged to be active in an institutional church. The atmosphere of the home groups was warm, inviting, and evangelistic. They reached out to street drunks, accepting them into their fellowship.

The foundations of the Oxford Group were the four absolutes: absolute honesty, absolute purity, absolute unselfishness, and absolute love.[9] Those who joined were invited to confess their sins in the context of the group fellowship. Individual Oxford Group members were asked to check the daily guidance they received by sharing it within the group fellowship. It was through confession, sharing, and belief in a Power greater than themselves that Bill W. and his friends Ebby and Dr. Bob were able to stay sober.

The Oxford Group spiritual way of life focused on the process of *metanoia*, a life turned back to God. This process goes through five stages: confidence, confession, conviction, conversion, and continuance.[10] There are five procedures: to give in to God, to listen to God's directions, to check guidance, to make restitution, and to share.[11] There are also six basic assumptions of the Oxford Group way of living: People are sinners, people can be changed, confession is a prerequisite to change, the changed soul has direct access to God, the age of miracles has returned, and those who have been changed must change others.[12]

The Oxford Group, now known as Moral Re-Armament, has lost its popularity but is still active in England.

The "A" Model

After six months of sobriety, Bill W. went to Akron on business and found himself alone in his hotel. The familiar smells and noises from the hotel bar enticed him to come in. He desperately searched for the nearest phone booth and began calling clergy to find an Oxford Group meeting to attend. After several phone calls an Episcopal priest gave him ten names. He called the first nine, with no luck. He was down to the last coin when Henrietta Seiberling answered the phone. She put him in touch with Dr. Bob Smith. Dr. Bob was just coming off his latest drinking binge, but agreed to meet Bill at Henrietta's house. There in her kitchen, Bill, Henrietta, Dr. Bob, and his wife spent hours together while Bill W. shared his story. Many cups of coffee later the urge to drink lessened for both Dr. Bob and Bill W. They had found the secret to one-day-at-a-time sobriety, another drunk to talk to. The trunk of the tree began to grow from its roots.

The early Oxford Group meetings resembled Quaker meetings, which had times for quiet and personal reflection. But the essential ingredients in these AA meetings were talking, listening to others talk, sharing stories over a cup of coffee, or calling someone met during the week. Just as in the Oxford Group meetings or the Boiler Room meetings, everyone was welcome and everyone was vulnerable — and a three-pound can of Eight O'Clock coffee cost only twenty-nine cents![13]

What the Oxford Groupers were hoping to do for the world, Alcoholics Anonymous hoped to do for drunks who wanted to stay sober. Like the Christian converts who had gone before them, these drunks became pilgrims along the way to sobriety. In the process they evangelized each other, giving each other hope, courage, and new strength, helping each other grow in purity, unselfishness, love, and honesty. Today these new converts meet in church basements around coffee, at fast food restaurants, or by phone. This talking, interaction, sharing of stories, and caring for one another provide the safety that enables them to admit to character defects of laziness, jealousy, willfulness, and resentments. To hear someone else say, "I did that when . . . ", or "I felt that way when . . . ", and "this is what helped me," makes you feel that you are not alone. "To be able to see the universality in your own experience is the key to how the program works," says Dr. Anne Geller, who directs the Smithers treatment center in Manhattan.[14] Addicts are protected by anonymity and forgiven in advance for relapsing. Isolated addicts are brought into relationship with others like themselves. For the first time they are able to look into the faces of others and see themselves. According to Damian McElrath, director of the Hazelden Rehabilitation Center:

> the problem with the active alcoholic (or addict) is that his life is a monologue — he connects with his addicted self, and that is all. Ninety percent of the recovery process is through peers talking with one another. The beginning of all wisdom is self-knowledge. In AA, you connect first with yourself. Then with another human being. Then with your Higher Power. You can't say, "I love God and hate my brother."[15]

Other Covenant Communities: Israel and the Church

Finding strength in community is nothing new; it is what God has always intended for us. But our American way of life has promoted rugged individualism instead.

"You shall love the Lord your God with all your heart, soul, mind, and strength and your neighbor as yourself." These are the great commandments of the Deuteronomic Code, found in Deuteronomy 6:5 and Leviticus 19:18. Jesus paraphrased them into one Great Commandment (Matt. 22:37–39, Mark 12:28–34, and Luke 10:25–28) and stated that following this commandment was all that was needed to live. Just as devout Jews honor God and the Ten Commandments, the early Christians took this Great Commandment seriously when they met in each other's homes to pray and break bread together.

Israel was the first covenant community, the early Christian church the second. The first record we have of such a Christian group is in Acts 2:43–47. Along with the recording of how these first Christians lived in community is the description of the healings and their attractiveness to others. These early Christians prayed together, shared their experiences of Jesus, and encouraged one another. "Unless there is some structured time for group sharing, people get lost and Christian love is not expressed," states Morton Kelsey.[16] As they shared their experiences and cared for each other, they also shared their community property.

During the Reformation the Anabaptist movement tried to recapture the commitment required by the People of the Way, as these early Christians were called. Today the Amish, the Mennonites, and others carry on the Anabaptist tradition, attempting to live the Christian way in community. The Mennonites, founded by Menno Simons, started as a house church movement in Zurich, Switzerland, in 1536. They too believe in a change of character followed by a change in conduct. They serve in the name of Christ in many parts of the world, caring and sharing with a sense of mission. There is a remarkable similarity between this early Christian and Anabaptist tradition of a covenant community and the "A" fellowship groups.

Twelve-Step Communities

The explosion of the "A" groups all over the country and now spreading to other countries indicates that people are starving for this kind of participatory, sharing community. The collapse of the family as a caring, nurturing unit, the depersonalization of society, and the failure of recreation and escapism to fulfill our deepest need for God and for each other are important factors explaining the phenomenon of the self-help movement. People are seeking a sense of identity, a sense of belonging. They have a deep need to share in each other's suffering and pain. Evelyn Woodward defines community as, "a group fired by a common vision."[17] Some attempt is being made in various denominations to encourage small group sharing and community building.[18] "The main goal of pastoral efforts in the Church today is to build communities which make it possible for a person to live a Christian life," says Stephen B. Clark, a member of the Cursillo movement.[19] The basic Christian communities of Latin America are another model.

What is required by God, asks the prophet Isaiah. And he answers, "To act justly, to love mercy and to walk humbly with your God" (Mic. 6:8). Justice is to meet our fellow human beings, sharing and supporting them in their suffering. It is the way God meets us, through the suffering and death of his Son, Jesus Christ.

Unlike group therapy, the twelve-step "A" groups do not seek to change anyone and there is no trained person in charge of the process. Group therapy tends to be more open-ended, where individuals learn to interact with each other on a feeling and response level. The group process of the "A" groups is based on support and encouragement. "Keep coming back, it works." No special therapy techniques are used. It does not involve psychodrama, role playing, cognitive therapy, or intrapsychic therapy. Although individual and group therapy have their place in the treatment of addiction, the "A" group fellowships are a form of *koinonia*. *Koinonia* is a Greek word that means community, or the close union or joint participation and sharing by individuals in each other's lives. They become related, in a sense a new kind of family, through a common need or a common problem. They learn how to live with the problem one day at a time, with God's help and with the help of the group.

New Rings Every Year

> On each side of the river stood the tree of Life, bearing twelve crops and yielding its fruit every month. And the leaves of the tree are for the healing of the nations.
>
> — Revelation 22:2 NIV

The archivist at Alcoholics Anonymous headquarters in New York City keeps track of the new AA groups with computers and a wall map with color-coded pins. In 1990, there were over 87,696 AA groups in 136 countries. One-third of the members were women and one-fifth thirty years old and younger. In the United States and Canada alone, there has been an estimated increase of 4,000 new groups a year, not taking into account another 1,200 groups that AA headquarters hears of indirectly.[20] In Seattle, Washington, on July 5–8, 1990, Alcoholics Anonymous celebrated fifty-five years as an international organization. Over 46,000 people were in attendance. The basic text of Alcoholics Anonymous is now being printed in various languages for each of the international groups. There are 30,000 Al-Anon groups in 101 countries and 3,500 Al-ateen groups.[21]

As these new rings are added each year, the recovery program begun by Dr. Bob and Bill W. in a kitchen in Akron has come of age. It is now a mature tree, with breadth as well as height. Like the cedars of Lebanon, it dominates the forest landscape. No longer is there a stigma to attending "A" meetings. It is the "in" thing to be in recovery. In the United States and Canada, there are sometimes more cars in the parking lots of churches on meeting nights than on Sunday mornings. In Eastern Europe and the Soviet Union Alcoholics Anonymous groups and some Al-Anon groups are mushrooming as church buildings are being reopened and people are looking for alternatives to the scientific/mental health approach to treating alcoholism.

Addicts and co-addicts of every shape, age, color, and nationality, reaching out to help each other, seem to be God's solution to binding up the wounds of the nations, bringing us back into community again, into fellowship with God and with each other.

3

THE TWELVE BRANCHES

The Significance of Twelve

> If God is going to move he uses number twelve.
>
> — Malcolm Smith

It is not a coincidence that Bill W. chose twelve steps for the principles of recovery incorporated by Alcoholics Anonymous. The number twelve has particular spiritual significance.

Meaning in Scripture

There are ninety-seven references to the number twelve in the Old Testament and fifty-four in the New Testament. The number twelve was sacred to the people of Israel. It was the number chosen for the twelve princes predicted in Genesis to father each of the twelve tribes of Israel. It was used to describe pillars of stone set up by Moses in the wilderness, the tribes of Israel (Exod. 24:4), the cakes commanded to be offered to the Lord by the Israelites (Lev. 24:5), the stones placed in the Jordan River by Joshua to prepare the Israelites to cross into the promised land (Josh. 4:9).

The number symbolized the people of God in their totality. Twelve represented not only the community of Israel,[1] which was made up of twelve tribes, but also completion. It had both a poetic and mystical sense to it. Twelve is also symbolic because it is a product of three, which is a heavenly number, and four, which is an earthly number, so it represents the totality of earth and heaven together.[2] The care of God's sanctuary was shared among the twelve tribes, each responsible for one month of the year. It was a very practical solution to the maintenance of the Holy Place of God. One might say that it was God's organizational genius to make sure that everything that had meaning in Old Testament times was symbolized by the number twelve!

It naturally follows, then, that Jesus would have selected twelve apostles (Matt. 10:1–5). He gave them a place of honor in his heavenly kingdom, as judges of the twelve tribes of Israel (Luke 22:30). The Epistle of James opens with a salutation to the twelve scattered tribes of Israel, dispersed throughout the world (James 1:1). After Judas betrayed Jesus and killed himself, his place was taken by Matthias to "complete" the number needed to carry on the work of Christ in the world. The twelve Apostles, one might say, became the foundation of the early Christian church. Today in some traditions, the Episcopal Church included, bishops are selected as part of the "apostolic succession."

Finally, at the close of history, the people of God, both Jews and Gentiles, are symbolized by the number 144,000, a multiple of twelve. The Apostle John, exiled bishop of Asia Minor chained to a wall in a cave at Patmos, writes in the Book of Revelation, the last book of the Bible, describing a vision of how it will be:

> So the Spirit carried me to a great high mountain, and showed me the holy city of Jerusalem coming down out of heaven from God. It shone like the glory of God; it had the radiance of some priceless jewel, like a jasper, clear as crystal. It had a great high wall, with twelve gates, at which were twelve angels; and on the gates were inscribed the names of the twelve tribes of Israel. There were three gates to the east, three to the north, three to the south, and three to the west. The city wall had twelve foundation stones, and on them were the names of the twelve apostles of the Lamb.
>
> (Rev. 21:10–14 NEB)

It is also symbolic that Jesus was twelve years old when he first appeared in Jerusalem, debating with the learned scribes and Pharisees in the temple. As Luke describes in his gospel, it was at that time that he was made ready for public service, even though his parents did not understand (Luke 2:41–52).

Significance to Bill W.

> I relaxed and asked for guidance. With a speed that was astonishing, considering my jangled emotions, I completed the first draft. It took perhaps half an hour. The words kept on coming. When I reached a stopping point, I numbered the new steps. They added up to twelve. Somehow this number seemed significant. Without any special rhyme or reason I connected them with the twelve apostles.[3]

Like the Apostle John, Bill Wilson was moved by the inspiration of the Holy Spirit to write the twelve steps of Alcoholics Anonymous. His experiences in the Oxford Group movement, directly influenced the formation of those steps. But it was several years into his recovery, after the fledgling Alcoholics Anonymous group numbered about a hundred persons in both Akron and New York City, before the original twelve steps were written down and then revised and put into their present form.

Irving Harris, in his book *The Breeze of the Spirit*, describes how Bill, after his commitment to Christ at the Calvary Mission and while attending Oxford Group meetings with his friend Ebby, discussed the precepts of the Oxford Group during the early stages of yet another detoxification at Towns Hospital. He asked Ebby to summarize those precepts for him:

> You admitted you are licked. You get honest with yourself. You talk things out with someone else. If possible you make restitution to the people you have harmed. You try to give of yourself without stint and with no demand for reward. And you pray to whatever God you think there is, entirely as an experiment.[4]

Later, in 1938, after he had met Dr. Bob, they sat up night after night while Bill was living at his home in Akron discussing the principles of the Oxford Group movement. For several months he tried to put down in writing how these principles "worked" to keep these early recovering alcoholics sober. This is what he wrote:

1. We admitted that we were licked, that we were powerless over alcohol.
2. We made an inventory of our defects or sins.

3. We confessed or shared our shortcomings with another person in confidence.
4. We made restitution to all those we had harmed by our drinking.
5. We tried to help other alcoholics, with no thought of reward in money or prestige.
6. We prayed to whatever God we thought there was for power to practice these precepts.[5]

While Bill was in the process of trying to encapsulize the "truth" about how the program worked, the early recovering alcoholics in New York were breaking away from their involvement with the Oxford Group movement. One of the issues was the "absolutism" or perfectionism of the Oxford Group's way of life. The four absolutes of the Oxford Group were:

Absolute Honesty: Both with ourselves and with others, in word, deed, and thought.

Absolute Unselfishness: To be willing wherever possible to help others who need our help.

Absolute Love: "Thou shalt love the Lord thy God with all thy heart, and with all thy soul, and with all they mind. And... thou shalt love thy neighbor as thyself."

Absolute Purity: Purity of mind, of body, and of purpose.[6]

These had been adopted by these early recovering alcoholics as the spiritual way to sobriety.

While Bill W. was in Akron with Dr. Bob, the New York City group of recovering alcoholics decided to split with the Oxford Group movement. Since the Akron group of recovering alcoholics was still actively participating in the local Oxford Group meetings, Bill W. was concerned about how his six steps would be accepted in New York because they were so close to the Oxford absolute standards. So he talked to Dr. Bob and made a decision that his six steps of recovery needed to more explicit. "There must not be a single loophole through which the rationalizing alcoholic could wiggle out."[7]

Even though they wanted to avoid perfectionism, they still wanted to keep the close fellowship experienced in the Oxford Group process. It had become important in maintaining their sobriety. That process is described as follows:

> There was complete informality and you could say what you liked, but the spiritual temperature was such that the dilettante and the armchair theorist soon found the pace too hot for him. People were blunt with themselves and each other. Absolute standards of honesty and unselfishness were applied not to some pleasant pipe-dream of the sweet by and by, but to details of the nasty now and now.[8]

The Inspiration of the Steps

> A pile of wisdom and experience is packed into the Twelve Steps. I have even compared the inspired 40 minutes during which those steps were given to AA's co-founder to the time in which the Ten Tables of the Law were given to Moses on Mt. Sinai. . . . It is an hour when men's powers are in high pitch and tension and when the Spirit of God hovers near, making suggestions.[9]

While Bill Wilson was in Akron pondering just how the principles of the program needed to be changed, he had an inspiration. This is what came him one evening after he had gone to bed. He got out a pad and a pencil and wrote:

> We admitted we were powerless over alcohol — that our lives had become unmanageable.
>
> Came to believe that God could restore us to sanity.
>
> Made a decision to turn our wills and our lives over to the care and direction of God.
>
> Made a searching and fearless moral inventory of ourselves.
>
> Admitted to God, to ourselves, and to another human being the exact nature of our wrongs.
>
> Were entirely willing that God remove all these shortcomings.
>
> Humbly on our knees asked Him to remove our shortcomings.
>
> Made a complete list of all persons we had harmed, and became willing to make amends to them all.

Made direct amends to such people wherever possible, except when to do so would injure them or others.

Continued to take personal inventory and when we were wrong promptly admitted it.

Sought through prayer and meditation to improve our contact with God, praying only for knowledge of his will for us and the power to carry that out.

Having had a spiritual experience as a result of this course of action, we tried to carry this message to others, especially alcoholics and to practice these principles in all our affairs.[10]

Many comments and much controversy surrounded this original version of the twelve steps. Many of those who had come into the program with little or no faith were concerned about how suffering alcoholics would perceive the "religious" nature of the steps. "You've got too much God in these steps; you will scare people away," two of Bill W.'s newly recovering friends reacted.[11] Bill Wilson held his ground amid the sea of opinions expressed as this original version made the rounds of recovering alcoholics for review. He eventually compromised on some of the wording about the concept of God, and the twelve steps finally were accepted as they are worded today.

The Steps and Christianity

My Grace is all you need, for my power is strongest when you are weak.

— 2 Corinthians 12:9–10 GNB

The Apostle Paul suffered from a painful physical ailment. Some scholars say it had something to do with his eyes. Others say it was a form of epilepsy. He attributes the ailment, whatever it was, to a way for God to keep him humble, from being puffed up with pride, for he had to contend with it daily. Three times, he says, he asked God to remove it from him. So he had to be content to be weak so that God could be strong. It became his stimulus to continue to do God's will and not his own. From the record of his fallouts with the other apostles, in particular Barnabas (Acts 15:36–41), we can surmise that Paul was strong willed.

But he had to live daily with, as he describes it, "a thorn in the flesh." It kept him from boasting, from spiritual pride.

Job too, like Paul, cried out, "How long will you torment me" as he struggled with a disease like leprosy (Job 19:1–7). He responded that even if it were true that he had been wronged, the error remained with himself. He refused to blame God or anyone else.

Alcoholics also have a physical ailment, a "thorn in the flesh," a biological predisposition, a craving for alcohol. They have tried hard to control their drinking; they have put the blame on others. It isn't until they give up their struggle and put their lives into God's hands that they find the strength, in their weakness, sufficient to live in sobriety and to get spiritual relief. The same is true for the co-addicts or co-dependents. When they stop trying to control the other's drinking (or other addictive behavior) and are reminded of their own powerlessness, they can find spiritual relief.

According to the testimony of many alcoholics and family members in recovery the spiritual way of restoration to fullness of life can best be summarized as:

TRUST GOD
CLEAN HOUSE
HELP OTHERS

As Tony (see below, p. 78) paraphrased the process, all twelve steps need to be followed in sequence if the addict is to receive the promised spiritual restoration. It is in following the twelve steps, in order, that one is restored into the wholeness of relationship with God and then freedom from the ravages of addiction. The twelve promises are these:

1. We are going to know a new freedom and a new happiness.
2. We will not regret the past nor wish to shut the door on it.
3. We will comprehend the word "serenity."
4. We will know peace.
5. No matter how far down the scale we have gone, we will see how our experience can benefit others.
6. That feeling of uselessness and self-pity will disappear.

7. We will lose interest in selfish things and gain interest in our fellows.
8. Self-seeking will slip away.
9. Our whole attitude and outlook on life will change.
10. Fear of people and economic security will leave us.
11. We will intuitively know how to handle situations which used to baffle us.
12. We will suddenly realize that God is doing for us what we could not do for ourselves.[12]

The Steps and Protestant Evangelical Christianity

Evangelical ministers from three major Protestant denominations had their influence on Bill Wilson and the formation of the twelve steps.

Almost fifty years later a director of the National Council on Alcoholism in Long Beach, California, Bob Bartosch, found that the twelve steps seemed to come directly from biblical references.[13] Since the first group of recovering alcoholics in Akron read the Bible frequently in their meetings, this is not really a revelation. In fact, the process of recovery is an age-old process of repentance and conversion. This spiritual way has been proclaimed throughout the scriptures, both Old and New Testament, as the way to *shalom*, wholeness, and completeness. The Al-Anon family program describes this spiritual way in their book *Al-Anon Faces Alcoholism:*

- Acknowledgement of our dependence on a Supreme Being.
- Love for our fellow man and recognition of his dignity and value.
- Awareness of the need to improve ourselves through self-appraisal and admitting our faults.
- Belief in the effective spiritual power of true personal humility and conscious gratitude.
- Willingness to help others.

These ideas are the very substance of the Ten Commandments, the Sermon on the Mount and the Golden Rule. The working phi-

> losophy of Al-Anon is a pattern for right living, for overcoming difficulties and for helping us to achieve our aspirations.
>
> We come into Al-Anon to solve the specific problem of alcoholism and its disastrous effect on our lives. We apply the basic spiritual ideas by means of what we call the Twelve Steps. These are reinforced by the Twelve Traditions, by the Serenity Prayer and by a group of concepts known simply as the Slogans. . . . These ideas contained by the words, applied to our daily lives, can bring about unimaginable changes for the better, but only to the degree that we absorb and use them.[14]

"But before God can heal our spiritual infirmities," says Grant Schnarr in *Unlocking Your Spiritual Potential — A Twelve Step Approach*, "we have to recognize them, admit that we have a problem, and ask for help."[15]

The process of healing and wholeness seems so simple; at least the early Christians thought so. To repent, believe, and be baptized was all that was needed to follow the Christian way of life. Over the centuries, the church has made it more complicated. In its attempt to "keep it simple," the church has creedalized, doctrinalized, and apologetized the Christian way. Like the Pharisees criticized by Jesus, it has "taken away the key to knowledge" (Luke 11:52). But the first recovering alcoholics rediscovered the key and addicts and their relatives have been rediscovering it to this day.

Other Christians over the centuries have discovered the same simple way to peace, health, and wholeness.

To begin the journey we have to come to a point of desperation or despair, to realize the human predicament that we are in is hopeless: "For I am full of trouble; my life is at the brink of the grave" (Ps. 88:3). Next comes the cry for help, "O Lord, my God, my Savior, by day and night I cry to you" (Ps. 88:1) and the question, "Are you there to help me?" Jonah found himself in the belly of the whale, up to his neck in darkness and water, when he finally cried for help. But all was not lost, as he discovered when the whale coughed him onto dry land. And so it is with us. Ezekiel 18 describes how the situation can change, how we can turn away from all our offenses and get a new heart and a new spirit (Ezek. 18:30–32)

The twelve-step way of new life is not a personal spiritual journey we make alone. It is not an "I journey" but a "we journey." Notice that the twelve steps begin with the pronoun "we" or "our" not "I" or "me." It is a journey made in community and in communion with others. The early recovering alcoholics did not have the twelve steps or the slogans to guide them but found that in community they miraculously were able to achieve sobriety and peace of mind.

Community was the key to Wesley's early Methodist group meetings as it is the key today for growth and vitality for individual church parishes in all denominations. Sam Shoemaker followed that model in his ministry, as was evidenced in the Oxford Group movement, the Pittsburgh Experiment, and Faith at Work. Christians actively involved in these groups, as well as others like Cursillo, making the commitment to hold each other accountable to follow a Christian way of life have been God's agents in renewing their churches.

The early recovering alcoholics took this Christian model, molded its precepts to help them stay sober, and found it worked.

The Steps and Catholic Mysticism

But there is another aspect to the spirituality of the twelve-step process, which Father Ed Dowling commented on when he mentioned to Bill W. how much it was like the Spiritual Exercises of St. Ignatius.[16] St. Ignatius comments that people who make marriage or acquiring wealth and material possessions an end tend to put God second in their lives, "only after their disordered attachment." "What they ought to seek first and above all else, they often seek last."[17] Addiction results. The attraction of "the disordered attachment" becomes more important than God or a spiritual way of life. Such an attachment leads to addiction.

Those who enter monastic life are under the tutelage of a spiritual director, who helps the novice through the process of following the Spiritual Exercises or rule of life. The sponsor in a twelve-step program serves a similar function.

Those involved in twelve-step recovery programs prefer to speak about spirituality rather than religion, about following a spiritual way of life rather than a religious way of life. It is the mysticism rooted in the Johannine writings in the Bible. These writings, attributed to the Apostle John and written in the later part of the first century C.E., were composed in the vernacular of a creeping gnosticism that by then was influencing not only the Roman world of the day but also the fledgling Christian house churches. It is this mysticism that has sustained Christianity in the Eastern Orthodox churches throughout the decades of Communist oppression. The danger is that this mysticism can either draw one apart from society and community into the isolation so dangerous to continued recovery for the alcoholic or addict or into self-centered humanism with its continuous struggle to achieve higher levels of a spiritual ideal. It tends to negate the prevenient and effective grace that is the essence of the gospel message.

The Hero's Journey

A clear distinction is made by those in the 'A' group recovery process that they are not "religious" groups but "spiritual groups. Morton Kelsey calls a religious person one who "not only needs experiences of the risen Christ but also needs to be an effective instrument of that power in the world. This heroism can be embodied in outer actions, in thinking, in scientific discovery, in religious practice, or in theological study."[18]

Following the twelve-step way to recovery is sometimes called the hero's journey, as found in mythology. It is a journey one has been selected by God to take, a journey that answers the big questions of life, a journey that leads to new strength and hope. On the journey the dragons are faced. These dragons are sometimes called the seven deadly sins; they represent greed, the binding of one's ego, the stuckness in old patterns of thinking, old habits of coping. The ego is tamed, the superego is released, inner talents and gifts are discovered and claimed and shared with others. The following prayer written by Dan M. and Jemima Shetler gratefully acknowledges the fruits and benefits gleaned from the twelve-step hero and heroine's journey:

> Thank you, dear God, for another day;
> The chance to live in a decent way;
> To feel again the joy of living,
> And happiness that comes from giving.
> Thank you friends who can understand
> And the peace that flows from your loving hand.
>
> Help me to wake to the morning sun
> with the prayer, "Today Thy will be done,
> for with your help I will find the way."[19]

"We came into A.A. to get sober and if we stay long enough, we learn a new way of living."[20] It is this new way of living that the twelve-step way of life provides, a way of life that involves honesty, conversion, and daily commitment. It is a way of life that has been statistically proven to provide personal contentment.[21]

The Steps: Simple Spiritual Truths and How They Work

Step 1: We admitted we were powerless over alcohol, that our lives had become unmanageable

Commonly known as the "surrender" step, this step is described by the Hazelden Treatment Program as the "foundation of recovery."[22] It is an admission of one's powerlessness and unmanageability, that as human beings we are unable to be fixed. We human beings are wholly unpredictable, infirm, and lame. It is only when we can admit our human condition or human problem that we can be repaired. So often our egos and our pride get in the way of God's ability to repair us and remake us in "his image." We cannot be molded by God until we have the willingness to be so, until we admit our weakness. It is so easy for addicts to blame others or rationalize their need to drink or use a drug. But that blaming behavior hides a deepening guilt:

> I know that good does not live in me — that is, in my human nature. For even though the desire to do good is in me, I am not able to do it. I don't do the good I want to do; instead, I do evil that I do not want to do. If I do what I don't want to do, this means that I am no longer the one who does it; instead, it is the sin that lives in me.
> (Rom. 7:18–20 GNB)

It is not wise or practical to advise addicts that if they would only try harder, they could quit drinking, smoking, or eating compulsively; in fact it reenforces the guilt. An outsider may know that the addict is out of control but the addict doesn't. The very nature of addiction is to mask the addicts' awareness of their behavior. Intervention and direct confrontation are important, because they are the only way addicts can know how they are behaving and how those surrounding them are responding to that behavior. Most addicts have a deep sense of moral conscience about wanting to do the right thing.

Step 2: Came to believe that a Power greater than ourselves could restore us to sanity

Step 2 goes beyond the despair and fear of the first step and gives hope. After taking step 1 it is tempting to wallow in our self-pity and continue to beat our breasts about the hopelessness of our condition. Alcoholics who tell at meetings the same self-story, or "lead," about the misdeeds of their past over and over never get beyond the first step. It is very easy to blame our disease on our parents' genes and to be defiant or resentful. It is tempting to remain the center of the universe even in our weakness or illness. It is depressing to think that no one can help us, not even ourselves.

God comes to us by invitation. He does not force his will on us even though he has the power to do so. We have the freedom to believe or not believe in God, to seek or not to seek a Power greater than ourselves. God takes the initiative and then leaves it up to us to respond.

But "everything is possible for him who believes," says Jesus (Mark 9:23). God help us in our unbelief! Unbelief only robs us of the promise of new life.

Step 3: Made a decision to turn our will and our lives over to the care of God as we understood Him

Here is where we get all mixed up in the doctrines of organized religion. Abraham Twerski says that "in many religions there are both fundamentals and trimmings."[23] We have all experienced others who have tried to push their beliefs down our throats. We may be bitter and resentful of well-meaning religious people who have done that to us. Or we may subscribe to a certain denominational way of thinking that says that if we just have faith enough we can stop our addictive behavior. But Alcoholics Anonymous says that all we have to do is believe in "a loving God as He may express Himself in our group conscience" and simply, to turn our lives over to this God.

The third step means that we have to move outside the center of the circle we have made for ourselves and to put God in the middle instead.

Alcoholism or any other addiction has been described as "self-will run riot." Turning one's self out of the center of the circle and putting God or even the group conscience or one's sponsor in the middle is not the American individual's way of doing things. We resent someone else interfering with our "inalienable rights" guaranteed to us in the United States Constitution. Many of us learned to survive in dysfunctional or alcoholic families by controlling ourselves and others. We learned not to trust others, only ourselves. Now we are being asked to trust some Higher Power, that we are not sure we even believe in. Yet this God says:

> I alone know the plans I have for you, plans to bring you prosperity and not disaster, plans to bring about the future you hope for. Then you shall call to me and come and pray to me, and I will answer you. You will seek me and find me because you seek me with all your heart. (Jer. 29:11–13 GNB)

Turning our will over to this God promises to be the turning point of our lives. This God, unlike human beings, always keeps his promises!

Step 4: Made a searching and fearless moral inventory of ourselves

This is the first action step needed to go beyond simple abstinence. It is difficult for all of us to admit our mistakes. Two common defense mechanisms are rationalization and projection. Scott Peck describes people who constantly lie and blame others as "people of the lie."[24]

Both *Alcoholics Anonymous* and Hazelden's *Guide to the Fourth Step Inventory* have detailed how a personal moral inventory is to be completed. It is a process of thorough self-examination, including personality defects, the seven cardinal sins, the Ten Commandments, virtues, attitudes, and responsibilities. This process is not just for alcoholics but for everyone every day. It should include both our assets as well as our liabilities. Sometimes assets can be liabilities or liabilities can become assets. The important thing is to expose them to ourselves and to God.

> God, where could I go to escape from you?
> Where could I get away from your presence?
> (Ps. 139:7 GNB)

Taking an inventory of ourselves is the first step toward self-awareness. It helps us get in touch with those parts of ourselves we would like to keep in the shadows. These shadows hide our resentments and our fears stemming from bitter hurts of the past.

The fourth step takes courage and time to examine our buried feelings. It needs to be specific and include the *who, when, where,* and *what* of each situation. Not only does it require thoroughness but also honesty (see Eph. 4:31).

Most of us want to avoid the discomfort of examining ourselves. It is helpful to have a gentle guide to carry us through the process.[25]

Step 5: Admitted to God, to ourselves and to another human being the exact nature of our wrongs

Step 5 is the action step toward freedom and a spiritual awakening. Note that it must be done to God *and* to ourselves *and* to another person. We may have a tendency to be too harsh on ourselves. We may have missed some important areas that we need to examine. We may be prone to scrupulosity, which is false guilt and puts us down instead of building us up. It is seeing sin in every temptation and shortcoming we experience. This means that we must have balance as we take the fourth step and, to accomplish this, sharing the inventory with another human being is very important.

For Roman Catholics the confessional has always served to reconcile us to God when we have done wrong. Protestants, however, consider a general daily confession adequate.[26] But the fifth step requires more. It requires a guide with whom one can share the moral inventory.

The guide needs to be someone who can be trusted and is respected, compassionate, and unconditionally accepting. A guide should be sensitive to our telling our painful story and help make us comfortable in the telling of it. Here are specific characteristics to look for in such a guide:

1. Must be able to keep confidentiality.
2. Must understand the process and be attempting to live by the twelve steps him- or herself.
3. Must be mature and wise and knowledgeable about addictions.
4. Must be willing to share personal examples and give feedback to your story.

This step takes not only courage but real humility and should be repeated whenever there is a need to do so — beginning where we left off.

> He who conceals his sins does not prosper, but whoever confesses and renounces them finds mercy. (Prov. 28:13 NIV)

In the early Christian church it was customary for people to confess their sins to one another and pray for one another so that not only would they be forgiven but they would be healed. This confessional process was basic also to the Oxford Group meetings and is still practiced in some churches today.

Step 6: Were entirely ready to have God remove all these defects of character

Now one comes face to face with God. Goodness doesn't count in this step; only honesty does. Again we must be willing to face our powerlessness and our unmanageability. Then we must be willing to allow God to have all our character defects, shortcomings, and misdeeds, which we have inventoried in step 4 and shared in step 5. Again it is a process of surrender, of shifting the load off our backs to God's.

> We have courage in God's presence, because we are sure that he hears us if we ask him for anything that is according to his will. He hears us when we ask him; and since we know this is true, we know also that he gives us what we ask from him. (1 John 5:14 GNB)

Step 7: Humbly asked Him to remove our shortcomings

Humility is a virtue few of us truly have, but without it we cannot grow in God's grace. To be humble is to live as close to the truth as possible. In Al-Anon humility often gets confused with self-humiliation. A true sense of oneself is without humiliation, grandiosity, or pretense. Only those who are willing to go through the pain of self-examination will find their reward. As in childbirth, that reward is a new life and a new freedom, a joy and a peace never experienced before.

> Humble yourselves, then, under God's mighty hand so that he will lift you up in his own good time. Leave all your worries with him, because he cares for you. (1 Pet. 5:6–7 GNB)

> He will forgive us our sins and purify us from all our wrongdoing. (1 John 1:9GNB)

Step 8: Made a list of all persons we had harmed, and became willing to make amends to them all

Now that we have restored our relationship with our Father in heaven it is time to restore broken relationships with fellow human beings.

The first part of this step is making a list. It should have specifics about those we have wronged or those who have wronged us. Our list might look something like this:[27]

AMENDS LIST

Person	Relationship	My wrongdoing	Effect on others	Effect on me
Joan	wife	angry insults	fear, anger	guilt, shame
Jane	co-worker	sexual advances at party	distrust, shame	loss of self-respect

There are three categories of wrongs for which we must be willing to make amends: (1) *material wrongs,* (2) *moral wrongs,* (3) *spiritual wrongs.*

Material wrongs are those tangible offenses that harmed people. Moral wrongs involve our inappropriate behavior that may have embarrassed or hurt people who have counted on us. Spiritual wrongs are those "acts of omission" or negligences to God, ourselves, our families, or our communities.

The very act of making the list helps dissipate the guilt. It also helps in sorting out our inappropriate guilt, often called shame, which is a sense of worthlessness that comes from abuse of others and leads to self-abuse.[28] Shame makes us consider ourselves bad and worthless because of our behavior. But God doesn't make junk, and we should never consider ourselves junk in the eyes of God.

The eighth step is a step toward maturity. As mature individuals and members of society we need to take responsibility for our actions. Mature persons do not consider themselves superior or infallible. They are willing to recognize their mistakes and make amends.

> Do to others as you would have them do to you. (Luke 6:31 NIV)

Step 9: Made direct amends to such people wherever possible except when to do so would injure them or others

Amends are not the same as apologies. Amends are made when we act differently from the way we did before. We need to make amends for ourselves, to ask for our own forgiveness as well as for the harm done to the other person.

We should make amends directly when possible. Suppose the person we harmed is too far away for us to speak directly to that person; we could write a letter. Suppose persons we harmed are deceased; we might give a donation to charity in their name. Suppose the persons we had harmed are still in their own active addiction; they will not understand if we make amends. They might even use it against us. What can we do then? We can pray for them or just treat them with respect when we see them, not reacting to their anger or inappropriate behavior, remembering that "there by the grace of God go I."

It is helpful to check out this amends-making process with our wise guide or sponsor. We do not want to use the last phrase of this step, "except when to do so would injure them or others," as a cop-out. But we want to make sure that our motives are to achieve at-one-ment, to feel good about ourselves and others, not harboring any resentments. The ideal is this:

> So if you are about to offer your gift to God at the altar and there you remember that your brother has something against you, leave

> your gift there in front of the altar, go at once and make peace with your brother, and then come back and offer your gift to God.
> (Matt. 5:23–24 GNB)

Our world is less than ideal, however, and we may have to make peace with our brother indirectly through God!

Step 10: Continued to take personal inventory and when we were wrong promptly admitted it

"Closed for inventory." We see this sign in windows of retail shops at least once a year. Yet how often do we take our own inventory? How often do we take stock of worthless and harmful attitudes and practices? For recovering addicts this inventory needs to be taken on a daily basis with God and periodically with a sponsor or special friend. The old attitudes of selfishness, dishonesty, resentment, and fear can easily creep back in whenever we are not on guard and upset our recovery. Also, the old messages that kept us in self-pity or with a poor self-image can come back when we are in familiar surroundings, for example, when we are with people who used to put us down. It is important to take a daily inventory of our thoughts, words, and actions promptly to deal with these shortcomings. Pride can be a very subtle sin, and we can mask blaming by openly admitting the wrong and then pointing out the other person's fault or justifying the wrong because of what the other person said or did.

As in the fifth step, it is important to share our inventory with another person and spend some time periodically to do some housecleaning of worn-out attitudes and actions.

> So, if you think you are standing firm, be careful that you don't fall. (1 Cor. 10:12)

Step 11: Sought through prayer and meditation to improve our conscious contact with God as we understood Him, praying only for knowledge of His will for us and the power to carry that out

Daily quiet time for prayer and meditation and seeking God's will for us for that day is the key to maintaining our recovery. We start with praising God and meditating on his greatness and mercy. Next we review our daily inventory, admitting our wrongs and asking for forgiveness. Then we thank God for working out his plan for us, asking him to make us open to being his instrument for that day. This may involve sharing our story, attending a meeting, or just listening to someone in need. Then at the end of the day we review the day and ask him to guide us through the night. According to St. Ignatius, the sixteenth-century Jesuit, it is this daily examination that puts everything in perspective.

Often it helps to start the day, and to end it, with some set prayers of daily devotional reading. This is the routine followed by those in monastic life. Orthodox Jews meet daily to study the Torah or Law and to pray and praise God. In the Anglican tradition, there is a lectionary for daily morning, noontime, and evening prayer. Roman Catholics can attend daily Mass. Whatever your religious preference or tradition, the important thing is to make daily time for God. It is essential for all of us in order to resist all temptations and to grow in God's Grace.

> Blessed is the man who does not walk in the counsel of the wicked or stand in the way of sinners or sit in the seat of mockers. But his delight is in the law of the Lord, and on his law he meditates day and night. He is like a tree planted by streams of water, which yields its fruit in season and whose leaf does not wither. Whatever he does prospers. (Ps. 1:1–3 NIV)

Step 12: Having had a spiritual awakening as the result of these Steps, we tried to carry the message to others, and to practice these principles in all our affairs

Dr. Bob stated that all the twelve steps, simmered down, resolve themselves into the words "love" and "service." Jesus says to all who wish to follow him:

> You know that the men who are considered rulers of the heathen have power over them, and the leaders have complete authority. This, however, is not the way it is among you. If one of you wants to be great, he must be the servant of the rest; and if one of you wants to be first, he must be the slave of all. For even the Son of Man did not come to be served; he came to serve and give his life to redeem many people. (Mark 10:42–45 GNB)

Not only is service the byword for Alcoholics Anonymous, but "carrying the message" to others is crucial to maintaining one's sobriety. This does not mean controlling the other person or forcing someone into sobriety. Not does it mean preaching at someone, for preaching often becomes judgmental.

Having a spiritual awakening is like removing a veil from one's eyes so that one sees clearly the hypocrisy, cruelty, and insanity of the world. Persons in recovery through twelve-step programs cannot understand why the rest of the world doesn't see things they way they do. Often it is a mountaintop experience; at other times it can lead to despair because it means giving up old friends and sometimes family members who don't see things the way we do.

It is helpful to remember that if we follow the twelve-step way to spirituality we become the chosen ones of God. Our light, if we keep the bulb clean and free from defects, can be a beacon to others:

> Let your light so shine before men that they will see your good works and glorify your Father who is in Heaven. (Matt. 5:16 RSV)

The Working of the Steps in Recovery

> The great things of life emerge out of small obediences. One thing comes from another; it is seldom let down out of heaven in its totality, but comes out of the simple obedience of taking one step at a time.
>
> — attributed to Helen Smith Shoemaker

Tony, the street evangelist, shares it in his story: the twelve-step recovery process works for those who are willing to work it, one step at a time. It is a process that begins with surrender and ends with carrying the message to others. William James said that the crisis of self-surrender has been and always must be the vital turning point of religious life. That surrender is what happens when one gives up control and cries, "help," as Bill W. did that day at Towns Hospital. For an addict, it means the willingness to do "whatever it takes" to begin the upward climb out of the abyss of addiction. It means being obedient to God's will. That obedience in a twelve-step program means first of all a willingness to attend AA, Al-Anon, OA, or other twelve-step group meetings. It means a willingness to allow a sponsor to direct the recovery process.

"It works if you work it" is a phrase often repeated at the end of twelve-step meetings. But "if you work it" might better be phrased, "if you allow it to work for you." Stubbornness and self-will, two character traits of addicts, stand in the way of working the steps. The prophet Jonah went far away from God's will for his life, which was to call the city of Nineveh to repentance. Reluctantly he finally made it to Nineveh, but not until he had found himself in the darkness of the belly of the whale! It isn't until alcoholics have been "swallowed" by their addiction and find themselves in the darkness and bleakness of the addiction that help is possible. It is called, in the language of the program, "hitting bottom." Then, not really wanting to do so, they attend a twelve-step meeting and God is able to begin to do the work of healing. But the emphasis is on God doing the work and not our working the steps on some kind of a ladder of success.

Abraham Twerski states that the twelve-step process to recovery is like an escalator, "a continuous chain, where eventually the uppermost step circulates and becomes the first step again."[29] Dave Else speaks of the process as a circular one, which begins again and again. Perhaps this is why the phrase "new beginning" is so often heard in twelve-step recovery.

Timing and patience are also crucial to the recovery process. Alcoholism, or any other addiction, is a disease of relapse, and going too fast in working the steps may be detrimental to long-term recovery. Sometimes an individual may take as long as six months to a year on the first three steps. Those first three steps are certainly crucial to ongoing sobriety and recovery. The obsessive compulsive nature of our addictive personalities is tempered only with time and patience with oneself in the recovery process.[30]

The twelve steps are meant to be twelve, not thirteen. One hears in twelve-step programs about the danger of the thirteenth step, namely the romantic attachments between sexes that occur because of repeated exposure to one another at twelve-step meetings. These relationships can be either heterosexual or homosexual. Alcoholics are notorious for substituting one addiction for another. Addiction to alcohol, another mood-altering drug, or food becomes an addiction to another person. Often abandoned by family and friends, desperately needy and hungry for love, an addict easily succumbs to the temptation to get "involved" in sexual liaisons with another person in the program. Abused women who are also chemically dependent, 40 to 60 percent of female addicts, are particularly vulnerable to this kind of addiction. The danger is that this relationship can become as destructive as the original addiction.

The twelve steps were intended to bring one back, on a daily basis, into a right relationship with God and with one's fellow man (and woman). This does not mean taking advantage or being taken advantage of to fulfill a person's pathological need. Fortunately, the current emphasis on co-dependency as a pathological condition throws some light on why addicts get caught in thirteenth-stepping.[31]

Even though our uniqueness and specialness as adopted sons and daughters of the "King of kings and Lord of lords" should predispose us to avoid being in unhealthy relationships, Christ's commandment "to love your neighbor as yourself" gets twisted to mean "I must do everything for the other person." The self gets lost, buried, and often abused in the process. Recapturing the jewel of one's uniqueness or specialness in the eyes of God is crucial to the twelve steps. That uniqueness and specialness are intended to be found in healthy relationships with others and a willingness for family members to be a part of the process of recovery too.

4

THE LEAVES, THE BUDS, AND THE FRUIT

The Big Book

> You will know them by their fruits. Are grapes gathered from thorns, or figs from thistles? So every sound tree bears good fruit, but the bad tree bears evil fruit. A sound tree cannot bear evil fruit, nor can a bad tree bear good fruit. Every tree that does not bear good fruit is cut down and thrown into the fire. Thus you will know them by their fruits.
>
> — Matthew 7:16–20 RSV

The sun streamed in the room and lit up the stained-glass window over the stage. A group of men and women sat in a circle in the front of the room. First they bowed their heads and repeated the Serenity Prayer. The leader of the group held a book in her hand and asked if everyone had a copy. They nodded, for they all had been given a copy of this book as they entered the room. The leader opened to a page and began to read. To some in the group the setting seemed vaguely familiar, a stirring of the not-too-distant past, in a Sunday school classroom, perhaps, when the leader of the group then had a Bible in her hand and the reading was a passage from the history of the Jews or from the history of the early church. But this time there was a difference. Now the leader was a counselor in a chemical dependency treatment center, and the story that she read or that the members of the group took turns reading was from *Alcoholics Anonymous*, or the Big Book, as it is commonly referred to by recovering addicts.[1] It has become a bible for those in recovery from chemical dependency.

There have been three editions of this basic text for Alcoholics Anonymous. The first appeared in April 1939 about the time Alcoholics Anonymous was founded, the third in 1976. The purpose, stated in the preface, is to represent the current membership of AA and to reach alcoholics. There are forty-four personal stories of those who have been in recovery for alcoholism. These are divided into three sections: The Pioneers (including Dr. Bob's and Bill W.'s stories), They Stopped in Time, and They Lost Nearly All. Because the early founders of AA knew that recovery begins when one alcoholic talks with another alcoholic, sharing his or her experience, strength, and hope, it was decided by the AA fellowship in the early days to write some of these stories down so that they would help others.

This basic text for Alcoholics Anonymous, placed at the beginning of the Big Book, describes the disease and recovery process. It is put together in a way to break through the denial and resistances of the addicts and their family members. Beginning with Dr. Silkworth, who treated alcoholics in New York City in the 1930s, among them Bill Wilson, alcoholism has been recognized and acknowledged by the American Medical Association, officially in 1956, as a treatable illness. Men and women drink, Dr. Silkworth states, because they like the effect produced by alcohol.[2] They become addicted to the alcohol. They cannot stop drinking without developing the phenomenon of craving. The only solution is through what he then called "moral psychology," which was called by William James in 1884 "participatory spiritual experience."[3] This knowledge of disease is the first information an alcoholic or an addict needs to know; the second is that there is a solution, a way out. The twelve steps are introduced in chapter 5 with a description of how they work, particularly step 4.

The first story in the Big Book is Bill Wilson's. Next come the stories of the original founders of Alcoholics Anonymous groups in various cities, followed by stories of those who have come into the program at various stages of their disease from all walks of life and all socioeconomic backgrounds, men and women, young and old. Doctor, salesman, housewife, lawyer, banker, waitress, socialite, minister's son, ex-con, and others all share the story of the progression of their disease and their recovery from it. They talk about personality changes and spiritual awakenings, each having recorded for others the changes that have taken place in their lives. By their willingness to share they are not only helping to keep themselves sober; they are encouraging others to face themselves honestly. Their stories have a timeless quality to them. They are ordinary people who have been given an extraordinary gift of recovery from their Higher Power. Some describe themselves as having been raised with regular church attendance. One southern farmer, an Episcopal minister's son, tells of his finding honesty and truth in this recovery.[4]

Each of the stories in the Big Book is representative of thousands of others, shared at Alcoholics Anonymous meetings everywhere. Like the stories shared in the original "Big Book," the Bible, they are being passed on by word of mouth to others. Each of these little sparks of light is lighting up the world and making it a better and healthier place to live for us all.

Shared Stories of Recovery

> Each tight little bud and leaf begins to open up as the entire plant turns to drink in the life-giving light of the Twelve Steps.
>
> — A. Philip Parham, *Letting God*

It seems that the last place to find out about the disease of alcoholism is the church, and yet it is the first place addicts or potential addicts turn when they are in distress. Our seminaries as well as our medical schools provide very little training on alcoholism and addiction, even though our nation has declared a "War on Drugs." Why is there so much denial? Why are institutional Christianity and Judaism not making such training mandatory for all ministers and religious leaders? These questions will be addressed more fully in the last section of this book. The Rev. David Else, past president of the National Episcopal Coalition on Alcohol and Drugs (NECAD), addresses these questions in an article in *Episcopalian/ Episcopal New Yorker* (November 1987). He stresses that in the church we have a complexity of issues, including clergy who are often co-dependent and in denial about their own chemical abuse and who are kept aloof from the laity. We also use alcohol in our religious and social rituals.

This chapter contains stories of recovering addicts and their family members who volunteered to share their stories and to express their opinions about how their church family helped or hindered their recovery process. All these individuals have been active in their churches since their youth. One was and still is in a religious community. The other three are lay persons. There are two Episcopalians, one Baptist, and one Presbyterian. Their experiences and their opinions may shed some light on the answers to the questions posed above.

A Clergy Daughter

My father was born, the second to youngest, one year before his father was elected and consecrated as a bishop in the Episcopal Church. My dad and his eight brothers and sisters grew up in the limelight of his father's position in the church, first as a clergyman and then as a bishop. As their mother was supportive of her husband's ministry and involved in the life of the church, my father and his brothers and sisters were brought up to reflect their parents' position in the church and the community. For example, they were not allowed to play baseball on Sunday because of what the people in the church would think. Their family life was to be an exemplary one for others, and daily family prayers and reading of scripture were important as well. My father and his brothers and sisters were raised by loving, caring Christian parents, and there was plenty of nurturing for each child as well as for the many visitors who shared their meals and hospitality.

My father, too, became an Episcopal minister, and I was born into the same clergy family tradition. I was the oldest daughter, my sister being five years younger. My father, like his father, was very busy in the church and in the community, but when he spent time with his family he carried on the caring, loving nurturing he had received from his family. And, as the tradition goes, in the three parishes where my father served my sister and I were expected to be the "good" preacher's kids, setting an example for others.

Dad not only inherited the clergy family tradition but also a disease, a disease that became full-blown by his late fifties. His younger brother's family had the disease too, but it had been diagnosed as diabetes and treated early. The disease came about because of a chemical imbalance having to do with the way sugar was metabolized in their bodies. My father's disease was related to diabetes and was diagnosed as low blood sugar. But in reality it was an insatiable craving for sugar, which finally got him in trouble with his use of alcohol. As his disease progressed he had blackouts and was then hospitalized.

He stopped drinking and began to attend an Alcoholics Anonymous meeting in someone's home. However, because of our position in the community and in the church, his disease was kept secret and not discussed until right before he died. It was, according to my mother, a disgrace for a minister to have this disease. Yet his preaching became inspired through working the twelve steps of the program, and he grew spiritually in the fellowship of others in the congregation who were involved in the twelve-step program too. But my mother would not attend Al-Anon meetings nor do anything about her recovery. She kept on with her own "controlled" drinking, putting my father to bed when he got into the booze again. She made sure that he fixed her drinks, as well as everyone else's.

I loved my father very much and couldn't accept that he had a problem with alcohol. My sister and I always believed that it was my mother's fault that he had a problem with drinking because she nagged him so much. He was the nice guy, but we were very angry at her. I remember my sister often saying to my dad, " Do something about her!" I was an adult with grown children of my own when the realization hit me that my dad was an alcoholic. It hurt. I had a favorite spot in the woods where I used to go and cry. Finally, I mustered enough courage to go to see a pastoral counselor. He suggested that I "try Al-Anon." But it took me a year to walk into my first meeting. After all, it was a small community and everyone knew my dad. I had presented an image in that community in raising my own family that I was such a capable person and had everything under control. The Girl Scout troop that I led called me the army sergeant, and I made sure that everyone was in line during the annual Memorial Day parade! I must have intimidated many of them, including my own children, for at times I took out all my anger and frustrations on them.

As an ACOA, I met and married a man who was a heavy drinker. His mother was an alcoholic, too. When our youngest daughter was in high school, my husband's drinking was getting out of control, our middle daughter was not eating, and our oldest daughter was using marijuana and alcohol. I used my special place in the woods often to deal with my pain, but I couldn't let anyone else know how I felt. With everything around me out of control, the "everything is fine" front didn't work anymore, and the perfectly controlled community and church leader became unglued. I knew I needed help but I didn't know where to turn. I put on weight, my menstrual periods where heavy, and diarrhea was an increasing problem for me. Finally, I got the courage to swallow my pride and attend my first Al-Anon meeting. It felt like coming home. The rigid defenses I had lived with for so many years began to fall away and I was open to the spiritual renewal process of the twelve steps.

Meanwhile my husband's drinking got worse, and he had a stroke. First the doctor said he couldn't smoke and he could drink only one or two ounces of alcohol a day. But he continued drinking and smoking. His black moods got worse. He became verbally abusive and had blackouts. I kept going to meetings and learned about detachment. There were suicide threats, the bill collectors called, and I began to set my boundaries. Our youngest daughter was in her freshman year at college and was staying out late at night drinking with friends at the local bars. It became more than I could bear, so one day I left home and checked myself into a local motel just to try to find my peace and serenity. I felt like I was being devoured by the alcohol disease.

We were attending a downtown church at the time. The minister had become a good friend of my husband's. He felt sorry for him after his stroke, and being a pastoral caregiver he and my husband often had lunch and a few rounds of cocktails at noontime.

My first attempt at getting help for our marriage was with a psychiatrist referred by a friend, but he didn't talk to us about my husband's drinking. He did say that my husband was putting me down verbally and he offered us valuable tips for improving our communication and sex life, but my husband was still drinking and threatening suicide. After a year of weekly counseling sessions, I made the switch to an addictions counselor. She helped me realize how sick my family was and helped me set my own boundaries.

My husband didn't like how I was becoming more independent, so he started coming to the counseling sessions with me and we began to talk about his drinking and my concerns about it. We had our first and only family session. Our oldest daughter, her dog, our middle daughter and her new husband, and our youngest daughter, a college student at the time, were all there. I was nervous and scared. I decided to start talking about my father's disease and his attendance at twelve-step meetings. Each daughter in turn proceeded to defend herself, deny the disease, and attack me. Our middle daughter was the only one to tell my husband that she had been concerned about his drinking and her own eating disorder. The therapist just listened and then pointed out to them that they were all angry at me. "Why?" I thought. "I have tried so hard to protect them from my husband's drinking, to be the perfect wife and mother." That session left me feeling more guilty, so I wrote each daughter a letter telling them how sorry I was that I had set such a standard of perfection and that I had been so controlling. But they didn't understand.

I did not want to move out of the house and knew my husband wouldn't move, so we began to sleep in separate rooms. My husband finally began to feel the pain, and one day our minister found him in the pew early one morning when he came to church. I received an angry call that he wanted to see me immediately. When I arrived at his office he sat me down and read me my marriage vows. Then, still feeling sorry for my husband, he took him to lunch and they bought a round of cocktails so that my husband would feel better. This intensified my guilt, making me more confused. I sought the help of another minister. At last, this time, I found someone who understood. He knew my story, because he had heard it many times before. He told the other minister that what he had said and done was inappropriate. In spite of that, my own wounds were deepened. I felt betrayed by my own minister, supposedly my spiritual guide and mentor. Back to the Al-Anon meetings I went to continue to work on my own forgiveness, a never-ending process. As a good clergy daughter, I had been trained to believe was that it was un-Christian to be angry and un-Christian not to be reconciled to your brother or sister, and that marriage was a life-long commitment.

Then my sister's husband called for help. Her behavior was becoming bizarre, and he didn't know what to do. My husband and I contacted a friend who did interventions, and he persuaded her to go into an alcohol in-patient treatment center. She stayed for a few days and then got a well-meaning friend to come and get her. She was too scared to come home, and instead went to New York City and picked up someone at bar and lived with him for a year. Her crazy, irrational midnight phone calls kept coming. After a year, her children finally convinced her to go to a mental health center, where she was evaluated as having bipolar depression and put on lithium. Meanwhile, she kept her booze in the car. She began to viciously attack me, demanding that her adult children not see me. I was hurt at first by the threatening letters. Everyone in the family focused on her sickness and bizarre behavior.

Meanwhile, our father was diagnosed with a terminal lung disease, and I played my comfortable role of the "good" daughter and the fixer, while my sister kept up her barrage of threatening letters and drunken phone calls. So I believed that it was my role to prove how good I really was, and I sat by his bedside when he died, promising to take care of my mother and assuring him that my sister would be all right, that he was not to worry about her. I did take care of my mother for awhile. She couldn't cope with my sister's sickness and my father's death. Her life patterns were set. Being the enabler and caretaker, I even reintroduced her to an old friend, a heavy drinker himself. They were married a year later and the pattern continued. She began drinking more heavily with him. When I became concerned about her drinking and driving, I told her so, and she isolated herself from me and turned to my sister instead. Sometimes I get an overwhelming feeling of oppression and panic when I know the two of them are drinking together.

Cut off from any maternal or fraternal relationships in my family of origin, I sometimes feel rootless. I shared the pain with our marriage counselor as my husband and I planted new roots in his sobriety. Gradually our relationship began to heal. Yet the pain of the losses in my relationship from my family of origin was reexperienced as I became aware of my adult children's drinking and eating patterns and I found myself again no longer able to cope and had to be treated for depression. I told my adult children my concerns and educated them about the risks of the disease. It seemed as if they didn't want to hear. I don't think they are as angry at me as they once were, but I don't know for sure because we still are unable to talk about it together without their being defensive.

I keep on in my own Al-Anon recovery program, attending open AA meetings, ACOA meetings, and CoDa (Codependents Anonymous) meetings as well. I try, one day at a time, to focus on my own recovery. Things are better for my husband and me, particularly as we experience the joy of being grandparents. I try not to dwell on the patterns of the disease passing on to them. I'm getting better at turning over those concerns to my Higher Power and in finding ways to help other families to break the cycle of addiction. But I still live with some of the pain. Occasionally the old buttons get pushed when I go back into familiar surroundings and situations and my emotions go haywire and my diarrhea returns. I have some diverticulitis, which is sensitive to stress, and arthritis in my back.

As a good clergy daughter, I had been faithfully disciplined since my childhood in prayer and service in the church. I had served as Sunday school teacher many times, as Diocesan Hunger Commission chairperson and Peace Commission chairperson. My husband was first junior warden and then senior warden. We brought our children up by attending church regularly each Sunday.

My first spiritual awakening had come as a teenager, while I was away at boarding school. In the back of my mind, for some time in my adult life, there was an unspoken desire to be a minister, but, since I was a woman, that was not encouraged. So I asked to be trained and accepted as a lay reader/chalice bearer in my church. Then I decided to further my education and training as a teacher/trainer, eventually founding a nonprofit environmental education organization.

My second spiritual awakening came as I began to work the twelve steps in the Al-Anon program. It was then that I realized that I was a controller and fixer, playing God. I had been doing all the fixing and care giving for him, or so I thought. The guilt was overwhelming, and I got down on my knees and gave over my will and my life to the care of God. But in doing so, I was not allowing his will to be done, but doing mine instead, trying hard to do everything right to change me. I still hadn't let go completely. My spiritual awakening gradually came as a result of this surrender process and working the steps. I found that the scriptures were coming alive for me. Not only did God speak to me through his Word but in the peace and serenity he showered upon me in times of pain. I have sensed his presence many times in my recovery process. I can only describe his presence as a marvelous source of energy, touching me lightly, infusing me with a love that still passes all my feeble attempts to describe.

I believed that I was experiencing some call for some special ministry. I went to see the bishop, and he encouraged me to be a part of a process for those seeking ordination. I turned over the organization that I had founded to others and started my seminary training after I was made a postulant for ordination. For four years I went through the process, two of those years at seminary, emerging with a degree in theology and biblical studies.

Meanwhile, my father died and my sister got sicker with the disease. My husband was sober for awhile, but then he started to drink again and I needed to set my boundaries. My family, who were still in their addiction, could not be supportive. The only person I could trust in the church was the minister who understood addiction. But it was my therapist and my sponsors in Al-Anon who provided the acceptance and nurturing that I needed to start to heal the wounds.

When my husband started to drink again I was in clinical pastoral training at a local hospital. I picked up the phone and called to set up an appointment with a lawyer, knowing that my marriage commitment was sacrosanct in my family and in the church. It was a very scary step to take. Then the same minister who had felt sorry for my husband and was one of his drinking buddies told me that the church had decided that I should not be allowed to continue in the process toward being an ordained minister. It felt like the rug was being pulled out from under me. My painful wounds opened again and deepened. But the experience of clinical pastoral training, a requirement for all persons who were in the process of ordination, had shown me that I had gifts for healing and pastoral counseling, so I began to take classes at a local pastoral counseling training session.

I knew that I was still called to be an ordained minister and that I needed to keep in a spiritual discipline, so I started to follow the rule of the Order of St. Francis and joined that order as a postulant. My husband and I made a geographic move, and I felt God calling me toward a daily morning prayer ministry at our church. There I was offered a job as a drug and alcohol counselor with the homeless living in shelters. The church was reviving the order of the perpetual diaconate, a servanthood style or model of ministry, and it seemed right for me. After all, wasn't St. Francis a deacon? And he took care of the homeless and the lepers. I told my boss that I considered myself to be a minister and that I would undertake the job as my calling.

Then I received a letter from my bishop saying that I could not call myself a minister and that the diocese would not endorse and support my ministry. One of those outcast homeless alcoholics had called to complain about me! Also, my mental health supervisors didn't like my talking to the men at the shelters about their drinking and drug use. Soon there were rumors that I was disrupting the lives of those in the shelters and I was chastised by my supervisors. Even though I was being successful in breaking through denial and getting men into treatment, the emotional abuse was too much and my health began to deteriorate. I finally quit, angry and frustrated, and with a bad back and increased gastrointestinal problems. The order of St. Francis decided that I was too angry to become a postulant in their order just as the church I had supported by daily prayer for two years decided that I had no call to be an ordained minister.

I was crushed but not beaten. I was devastated but not destroyed. I felt rejected but not forsaken. I went back to my meetings. I went back to my seminary professors. I called my old bishop. I went back into counseling. I went into group therapy to deal in a constructive way with my anger. Was I wrong? Was I sick? Was I crazy? Then I went back to my new family — my Al-Anon home, where I could be accepted and be comforted. One night I woke up startled because I was in the midst of a bed of snakes. Another time I woke up in the middle of the night with a tremendous sense of the presence of Christ. He was rocking me and holding me. I knew that I could not cut myself off from the church because it was his Body. I knew he had been crucified and resurrected for me and my pain began to heal.

My strong faith in Jesus Christ carries me through the pain and gives me hope. But my perceptions of the Body of Christ, the church, are more realistic. I've accepted that it is both human and divine, today more caught up in its humanness than its divineness. I mourn that it will not train its ministers to recognize and treat addiction. They are often addicted themselves. I mourn because so many clergy families are suffering like mine did with a disease. I mourn that the twelve steps self-help groups are taking over the mission of the church.

Every day, I fight the temptation to leave the church, to stop going there to worship God, and I find that some phases of the New Age movement are beckoning. I am discouraged about the clergy and the lack of a sense of a caring community in the church and much ignorance about the disease of chemical dependency. I almost feel like an outcast because of the disease. I live with the pain of rejection from both the church and my family. I sometimes have a hard time putting principles before personalities and need to be reminded that my twelve-step program says that it is the disease of alcoholism I need to be angry about and that I can help only those who are open to receiving the new life that I have been privileged to receive. Many of our old friends, our old drinking buddies, have deserted us. Even though we still invite them to visit us, we no longer serve alcoholic beverages and they find excuses not to come. I used to be a very trusting person, but I don't trust easily anymore. So I keep going to my recovery meetings because there I can work on my own forgiveness, still that unending process, and find that I do not need to continue to be so hard on myself. It is at twelve-step meetings that I feel love and acceptance and I can call someone when some of the old feelings and ways of behavior return. Perhaps now I have found the real church after all.

A Street Evangelist

Hi, my name is Tony and I am an alcoholic. I first started drinking when I was eleven years old. My father died then and my mother remarried. It wasn't long before I was also periodically using other drugs, too. I dropped out of school and held several janitorial positions, which I subsequently lost because of public drunkenness. I was cut off from my family and wandered on the streets of Pittsburgh, where I was a frequent visitor to the shelters and local soup kitchens.

I began attending AA in 1977, when I was eighteen years old. When I was six months sober and attending AA meetings, I was staying at the East End Cooperative Ministry Shelter in Pittsburgh. I picked up a Bible while I was there, and it was like "eating" the words off the page. I really hadn't understood the first three steps of the twelve steps when I began attending AA. But after I read the Bible and the "Big Book," they made sense to me. I accepted Jesus Christ as my Lord and Savior. I continued to go to meetings for the next eight months. But I was afraid of what other people would think about me, or that they wouldn't accept my conversion story, so I stopped going to meetings and stopped sharing with others. I was really having a problem relating to other people there. It was then that I started drinking again. My drinking got so bad I began to have seizures. The doctor told me I had epilepsy.

For the next seven years all I did was drink. Periodically the booze gave me the courage to go to the local soup kitchen to share my faith in Jesus Christ. I wanted to convert everyone. In between drinking bouts I would try AA again. It was late summer of 1986. I hadn't drunk for two days and was ready to jump off one of the bridges on the north side of Pittsburgh. I found myself, instead, at the Light of Life Mission on W. North Avenue on a Monday evening. I joined the men filing in off the street about six o'clock, and we took our places in the chairs as the evening prayer and praise service was about to begin. One of the outreach counselors asked if any of us needed help, and I got up the courage to go up to her and ask if she would pray with me. I told her I was an alcoholic, and she asked if I would be interested in going to the local hospital to be detoxed. Another man asked for help, too, so we drove with her to the hospital emergency room. We sat there for hours until they had seen everyone else. When only the two of us and the outreach worker were left, they called us in to be examined. The other man didn't have his medical assistance card with him so he was refused admittance. But I did. When they found out that I had a history of seizures they admitted me.

After the five-day detox period, I couldn't get into the Bridge Housing Rehabilitation Program at the mission because they were full. They wanted to send me back out onto the streets again. But the outreach worker who had brought me there found a place for me at a personal care boarding home for the elderly and suggested I attend AA meetings daily and get into some regular out-patient counseling.

I was unhappy at the nursing home because I couldn't relate to many of the other residents. I wanted to share Jesus Christ with other at the home, but there was only one elderly lady who was interested. I felt the others laughed at me for "preaching" about Jesus. Sometimes I just hid myself in my room with my Bible. The outreach worker visited me there and encouraged me to get to meetings and we shared about Jesus together. But I often was depressed and felt like it wasn't worth living. One day I got into a fight with one of the other residents, and the nursing home asked me to leave.

By the grace of God, there was a space open in the mission's Bridge Housing Rehabilitation Program. It became my home for almost a year. There I could talk about Jesus Christ and the staff accepted me. I received the appropriate support to keep in recovery. I continued in out-patient counseling and helped start an AA meeting at the mission. I was able to work the steps, but I sometimes jumped to the twelfth step too fast, because I still wanted to help others and run things at the mission. I had to learn to follow their strict regime at the mission, interact with others, and to deal with my rebellion to authority. I had several seizures early that year and had to be rushed to the hospital, but they tapered off as soon as the alcohol and other drugs disappeared from my body.

One time I got fed up with life at the mission and checked myself into the Arc House, another rehab program. They told me I was being rebellious to their rules and asked me to leave. So I went back to the mission, a little more humble than before. They were kind, but honest with me, making me see that I was coming across as judgmental and superior in the way I related to people. I listened this time. I decided just to do what I was told and try to make the best of it. I could relate to the director of the program, because he was a minister and I felt that I was called to be a minister, too. I joined the local Baptist church and talked to the minister there about what it would take for me to be a minister. Jude 20–23 was one of the many passages of scripture that really inspired me then:

> Build yourselves up on your most holy faith; pray in the Holy Spirit; keep yourselves in the love of God; wait for the mercy of our Lord Jesus Christ unto eternal life. And convince some, who doubt; save some by snatching them out of the fire; on some have mercy with fear, hating even the garment spotted by the flesh.

I gradually found that I could best provide encouragement and support for others in the program by sharing the twelve steps, the Big Book, and my story. That seemed best to help them over their crisis. In six months I was chairing my first meeting. I began to feel accepted as part of the mission family. When I felt rejected or bad about myself or had trouble with the authorities at the mission I talked it out with my counselor. I began to attend spirituality weekends for AA members at a local monastery.

While at the mission I completed my high school equivalency diploma. Then I moved to Wood Street Commons into my own apartment. Attendance at AA meetings became my lifeblood. I started taking two courses at the local university but found that the reading load was too hard for me. So I am now looking for a job.

My faith in Jesus Christ is growing. I am able to love people more and accept them the way they are, just as I was accepted at the mission. I am able to be responsible for myself and for others. Being a part of other people's lives is the most important thing in my life right now. I am very active in AA service, responsible for twenty to twenty-five groups in the area. I give leads and share at meetings. This is where God wants me to be, carrying the AA message to those who need it. The twelve steps work, if you work them in order.

The Sunday School Teacher and Choir Member

"Hi! My name is Marie and I am a miracle." This is how I introduce myself at twelve-step meetings. Over a thirty-year period, I had become sicker and sicker, physically, emotionally, and spiritually, with my addictions.

I considered myself to be a religious, pious person, loving God and others. I was kind and generous — outwardly a Christian — teaching

Sunday school singing in the church choir, visiting the sick and those in prison. Yet, the sicker I became, the more I seriously questioned the "Christian" example I was setting. Often I had heard that the First Commandment said, "Thou shalt have no other Gods before me" and in the New Testament that Jesus says to "love our neighbor as ourselves," but because of the guilt and shame resulting from my addiction, I found it difficult to love myself or my neighbor the way God would have me love.

When I became aware something was wrong, I was in real pain and I made the rounds of psychiatrists, psychologists, assertiveness classes, religious retreats, medical doctors, ministers, and priests. I believed that God would heal me, so I read many books about religion, psychology, self-esteem, spirituality, and secular improvement. I attended charismatic conferences and healing services and had hands laid on me many times. Sometimes I found temporary relief and it made the pain more bearable. I developed friendships, some of which later proved unhealthy.

I prayed to God as I had understood him as a child. I heard he was loving. How could this God love someone who knew what was right and wrong and yet continued to do wrong? Paul's words in Romans 7:15 — "I do not understand what I do; for I don't do what I would like to do, instead I do what I hate" — were real to me. I had so much shame and unworthiness I was stuck in my religiosity. When the priest at the Eucharist said that "we are not worthy to receive Jesus," I was sure it meant me. I was a "doer" for the church and yet I could never be "good enough" for God. When I was a teenager, I told God I would be a missionary to please him and felt guilty because I became a teacher, wife, and mother instead.

What I didn't know then was that I had inherited a family disease of abuse and addiction, the "sins of the fathers," passed on to me by genetic and environmental predisposition. As a child I was abandoned by my mother (in reality my sister) and was raised by a cold, stoic, puritanical grandmother. I was told that my father died when I was born, but in reality I was illegitimate. My brother-in-law, or uncle, sexually abused me. As relatives came and went, there was increased drinking and loud screaming. It was scary and disgusting and sometimes I had to flee the house to feel safe. That was what my early childhood was like.

The food I ate became a way to ease the pain. I played games with an uncle who weighed 240 pounds, trying to eat more than he did. I would eat a whole pie and then force myself to throw up. I added water to Coke bottles to cover up the pop I drank and took as many as a dozen candy bars with me when I went to baby sit.

Meanwhile, I was a model student and church worker. Even while I was giving talks against alcohol in school, I began to sneak alcohol from my uncle's bar. I joined them in drinking beer when I was with them. It was while I was in high school that I got my first high from diet pills. The good feelings made me feel normal. I escaped from the pain at camp, school, and church. A minister and his wife extended their friendship and that helped ease the pain. My church encouraged me to go to a church-related college and study music. There the diet pills came in handy to study all night. I didn't drink at college because it was not allowed. Codeine eventually joined diet pills for relief from menstrual cramps and would help me sink into oblivion.

Even though at thirteen I found out about my illegitimate birth, it was during my sophomore year in college after a confrontation with my birth mother that I was so upset that I was put on antidepressant pills. But I wanted to keep from upsetting my grandmother so I kept secret the suicidal feelings, the binges, the sneaking alcohol, the sexual abuse. I found after experiencing a religious high that I again felt depressed and empty. I felt physical pain when people tried to touch me and yet I wanted to be touched. It was so confusing! But I couldn't talk about it.

Although the people in the church tried to help, sometimes it was positive and sometimes negative. Sometimes the feelings of being alone were overwhelming. One such occasion was six weeks after my first year of teaching. I took a large overdose of tranquilizers and antidepressants. Even though I knew suicide was a sin, it really didn't matter. I was treated for depression in a local hospital, but that didn't stop me from more years of self-medicating, often using other people's pills, combining them with alcohol. I received psychiatric treatment through it all. I lived what appeared to be a "normal life," married, had children, went to P.T.A. meetings, served as club secretary, breast-fed my babies, while taking Librium, Elavil, and codeine! My disease was so cunning and baffling that I would switch from one drug to another, one doctor to another, so that I could take several prescriptions simultaneously. I sought the magical cure, always praying to God, but completely oblivious to the fact that the drugs had become my gods. I continued to receive treatment from physicians for my emotional outbursts. I fought with my children. I was treated for paranoia, depression, postnatal depression, low blood sugar, migraines, and finally post menopausal symptoms. But their treatments offered only temporary relief. So I became angry at God, at the church, and at the therapists and physicians.

During this time the Episcopal priest in the church I attended was most supportive because he gave me unconditional acceptance. He suggested that I start working the Overeaters Anonymous program and that I write two pages and make amends to myself. He allowed me to swear at God. Then I discontinued using Elavil, still not realizing that I was addicted. The priest left and my migraines continued. (I was still using codeine and phenobarbital.) A new therapist told me that I was just "retuning" my life. Even though I believed her, I wondered why I still felt so bad inside, was afraid, still had bouts of depression and headaches, and still needed pills for anxiety. The pain intensified and I applied to a pain clinic. But there was a long wait. I threw up in between my classes and finally became a "couch potato."

Meanwhile, encouraged by a friend who was in recovery, I registered for an ACOA therapy group. An hour before I was to be at the class, I lay on my bed crying. I looked up at the picture of Jesus by my bed and cried out, "Please, Jesus, help me!" I drove myself to the hospital, while under the influence of all the drugs I was taking. There, they took a routine drug and alcohol history, and I was admitted to the chemical dependency unit with the counselor's arms around me. I had taken step 1, admitting my powerlessness over drugs and that my life had become unmanageable.

I had no idea how encompassing my addictions were, but I knew I was sick and believed that I could be helped. It was a new beginning; my prayers were finally being answered. God was on the Cross through Jesus, but his Spirit was in the detox unit with me. The physical pain, the extreme emotional swings, and the spiritual pain were too much to bear alone. One night, unable to sleep, I looked out the window. The spotlight was on the entrance to the hospital. Still wondering whether I was crazy or whether it was all a joke, I saw above the hospital a large bird with the hospital spotlight shining on it. It hovered there, a beautiful white dove, a sign from God saying, "Marie, you are in the right place." A week later, I saw two birds hovering over the hospital entrance. Just a year ago, I had been told, another patient had left the hospital and taken an overdose of pills to end his life. This night I knew that the other bird was saying, "You are going to make it." The last day in the hospital, thirty-one days later, I woke to see only one bird. The beam of light made it look silvery and sparkling. It flew higher and higher, its wings outstretched. I knew then that everything would be okay. I shared the next day in my group counseling about my experience of hope. After that the images of the birds were gone. The spotlight had burned out. I believe that the dove was my special sign that God would always be with me and my recovery continues to this day.

It was the chaplain in the rehabilitation unit who helped me deal with my anger and pain from the past. His visual images of Jesus permeated my body and mind. I even experienced my father's arms around me. One night I came home and felt a presence surrounding me. The feeling of warmth, safety, peace, and love lasted for two hours. I found healing with a finality that I had never known before. I could at last let all the pain and anger go.

When I came home from the hospital I went first to my church. It was a Tuesday afternoon and not many people were there. A priest met me and told me that it was good that I was well. I flinched and ignored the fact that he neither knew nor understood that I would never get well, that I would always be an addict. Since the beginning of my recovery, I have felt much pain and disappointment in my church. Most people did not know why I had been in the hospital even though my name had been on the prayer list. People did not mention my illness, but I needed to talk about what had happened to me. The groups that I had belonged to did not send flowers or even a card, even though a few individuals did. I felt abandoned by the very group of Christians I needed and wanted to be with.

But I found in the twelve-step program what I did not find in the church, so I stopped attending church services. When I mentioned to the minister that my daughter would need support now that she was in recovery, he did not seem to identify. There were not many in my church who understood my struggles to stay clean and sober and sane those first six months in recovery. None of the clergy had any training in chemical dependency. When I went to visit other churches, I found twelve-step meetings instead. I miss the Eucharist. I look for spiritually oriented clergy and groups. I go on twelve-step retreats instead of going to church.

I believe that the clergy in the church are enablers of the disease of addiction. They provide loving care and not tough love. They are indifferent to the needs of addicts because they're not trained in chemical dependency, the addictive process, or recovery. If people had not excused some of my inappropriate behavior, I might have recovered sooner. If clergy had not allowed me to manipulate them, I would have recovered sooner. I wish clergy would take advantage of all the training on addiction provided by chemical dependency specialists. I ask them to encourage recovery through twelve-step support groups as well as through the healing powers of Jesus and the laying on of hands. The twelve-step program is essential in recovery from addiction.

One day, one well-meaning church lady told me that it was the devil who was in the twelve-step program. I prayed that the path of recovery I had chosen was all right. Then I sensed the loving presence of God surrounding me and knew that was where I needed to be right then. I still suffer from periodic bouts of depression and so does my daughter. But I feel accepted and loved by my sponsor. She continues to act as the loving presence of Jesus, accepting me where I am. Each day that I am sober and clean, God works through me. Today I can be a witness to my recovery and my faith on a ministry team in a local prison.

Today I do not have to use, I do not have to be perfect. I feel comfortable in my own skin. Today there is a God around me, between me and others, and within. Today I am clean and sober and relatively sane. I am a miracle.

The Church Outreach Worker

On my way into the jail, on a crisp afternoon in late September, I tripped and almost fell flat on my face. I knew that I had gone too far. I needed to slow down.

Slow down? Now? As chairman of the Outreach Committee of my church, in a suburb of New York City, I had reason to be proud of my latest accomplishment. Under my leadership, the Stewardship Committee had raised the level of pledges by over 10 percent. I had voted with the slim majority of the Session that voted to establish a women's shelter on church property. I had arranged the car pool that picked up the handicapped adults who would eventually join our congregation as full members. Now I could add the reorganization of the county jail ministry to my list. Why stop while I was on a roll?

Simply because as I entered the jail at two in the afternoon, I was in no condition to do much more than mumble my way through the service that I was there to lead. I was staggering drunk. I did not have a drinking problem. I was just overworked. There had not been much time, after singing in the choir that morning, to get home, have lunch, dress "down" for the afternoon service, and head for the jail. There had not, in fact, been time for lunch at all. Just time for a martini — or, in this case, four. Too fast, I told myself, and on an empty stomach. That was why they had hit me this hard. It was really not my fault.

If God wanted me to be sober, let him guide me! How many times had I knelt, hung over and remorseful, asking him to intervene in my life? Yet not once had I been given the slightest sign that God cared — or even listened. I had done so much, and what had he done? Zip! I didn't know why I should bother to work for him. He certainly was not working for me. I might as well quit, for all he cared. I would live my life in my own way. Adaptability, that was it. Adapt to changing circumstances. It's okay to drink, so long as you can control it, and I was controlling my drinking perfectly well. In fact, I had promised myself that if drinking ever interfered with my health, my family, or my job, I'd do something about it. And I had kept my word. When the aspirin that I took every night to reduce my next-morning headache began to upset my stomach, I stopped taking it. Better a blinding headache than a broken promise.

A few weeks later, in early October, I was demoted at work. It was okay. The president of my small company had a paternal attitude toward all his employees. While "reducing my administrative load," as he put it, he wanted me to know that I still had his confidence. He proved it by increasing my salary. Nowadays, I would call that a mixed message, but back then it was a cause for celebration. I started to celebrate on Friday evening, and was lying on the floor, unshaved and still celebrating, when the boss stopped by unannounced on Saturday afternoon. He was worried. He explained to my wife that I might have misunderstood the reasons behind my job change. He had to be sure that everything was okay at home. I was celebrating so hard that I could not get to my feet. He took that as a sign that I was more upset by the demotion than I had let on. He sat at the kitchen table and solemnly explained to my wife that I had been transferred, not demoted. Lying there on the floor, hearing his words through my alcoholic haze, I began to wonder if I had made a mistake. These thoughts went through my head: "What if he noticed that I sometimes drank a little too much? I had better control it for a while. I would start at the earliest opportunity — tomorrow. Wait up now, tomorrow was Sunday. No point in ruining a perfectly good weekend. Wait until Monday."

Come Monday evening, having nobly refrained from the lunchtime drink, I sat down at home and mixed myself a single cocktail. One was all I planned to have. I savored my Rob Roy like a connoisseur, as though it was the last drink left on earth. Man, was that good! Too bad that I could not have another. I could enjoy and afford the taste of fine liquor, so surely I deserved more than one. No matter that in fact I was drinking the local discount store brands. But a deal was deal. Only one, remember?

Waking the next morning to my usual fierce headache, I knew that at some time during the previous evening I had lost my determination to control my intake. I went from headache, to remorse, to the rationalization that yesterday was a trial run. This evening would be the first *real* demonstration of my iron-clad control.

Somehow, Tuesday's single drink developed into a blackout. So did Wednesday's and Thursday's and . . . by week's end, I was frantic. Somewhere after the first sip, my good intentions always disappeared. I drank heavily over the weekend — what difference did it *really* make if I went to church anyhow — while I tried to think through my mistakes. Where did I lose control? Tomorrow I would do it right!

By Thanksgiving week, my state of mind was worse than it had ever been. It had to be something that I was doing wrong. The holiday found me sloppily drunk — too much so to carve the turkey, or even sit at dinner for the whole meal. Who cared that the family had gathered? It did not matter whether I was there.

Things were already as bad as they could get. As Christmas neared, I saw that I was wrong again. Things were getting even worse. Could it be that I had a drinking problem? But I would lick it. I would!

We were invited to a New Year's Eve party, but my wife didn't want to go. I argued at the top of my voice, until she changed her mind. That party could be important. I was a home drinker. I would never disgrace myself at a friend's house. By staying sober there, I might find out why I could not do it at home. At the party, I was extremely careful. I made an excuse to mix my own drinks, with very little liquor. I stood around, making small talk in spite of the screaming in my head. I was so taken up by the effort, that when midnight came, I hardly noticed. It was not until about 12:30 a.m. that I looked at my watch. I *had made it!* I was *sober! Cold sober!*

I deserved a reward, so I slipped away from the group and headed for the kitchen. That's where they found me. When my host offered to drive me home, I insulted him. When he tried to take my car keys, I swung at him. I may have stormed out of his house. But I have to rely on the testimony of others: I was in a blackout. I woke with the sun streaming through the window. I was home, in my own bed, with no memory of how I got there. It began to come back, the incredible tension of the early evening, my joy at finding that midnight had passed . . . and after that, nothing. Had I made it? I turned my head, oh, so carefully and faced my wife. "That was quite a party!" She glared at me. "How would *you* know?" What I knew was that once again I had failed.

I could not deal with one more failure. For most of the day, I sat in my robe, staring at the wall. Around dusk, I reached a decision. I could not do it alone. I would get help. That night I went to bed sober for the first time in several years.

The road to recovery was painful. I did not know where to start. I knew of AA. Somehow a copy of the Big Book had appeared in our house months before. But what could I expect from a group that focused on God? He had been of no help thus far. Resolve kept me sober for a few days, and soon I was seeing a counselor who specialized in alcoholism. (In 1976, before the Betty Ford clinic, such people were rare.) Finally my counselor challenged me to go to an AA meeting.

I stood outside the door leading to the church basement. Could I go through with this? As I wavered, a tall, slim woman came by. "Are you coming in? All the best people are inside!" Slowly, with a tight feeling in my chest, I followed her down the steps and found that I was home.

I had no problem with the first two steps to recovery. I had no doubt that I was powerless over alcohol. Absent a Higher Power to help me, I was utterly destitute. I accepted the third step. Slowly, patiently, a group of strangers led me into warm personal relationships that I never thought were possible — with them, with God, and, after many months, with myself.

It was in many church basements that I have stayed sober over the years. My health has been restored. My life has been given back to me. God was at work after all.

A Monastic

I was born and raised in the Pittsburgh area in a very ethnic, Catholic neighborhood. I am the oldest of two children. There was a lot of drinking in our family and neighborhood. I would say that most of the families in the neighborhood were dysfunctional with heavy drinking like mine. Both my paternal and maternal grandfathers were alcoholics. My father rarely missed a day's work even though he drank heavily every day. My mother was handicapped from the age of seven, yet always cooked and took care of our family's needs even though we had very little money because most of the money my father brought home went to pay his bar bills. My sister is five years younger than myself and is not an alcoholic.

There was a lot of dissension in our house as well as anxiety and fear. There was physical, emotional, and verbal abuse. With the help of the AA program I am able to look back on my childhood and see that I was acting out with alcoholic behavior as a child. One of my earliest memories is my first day of school. My uncle took me to the local parochial school and I ran out when he left because I was so scared. I was smart but learned only what I was interested in learning. I compared myself to everyone else, and I was either not good enough or better than the others, striving for perfection and not wanting to make waves. I was popular but always on the fringes of trouble. When my mother gave me money for special offerings, which were collected periodically by the nuns, I would use it to buy candy and sneak it into class. I was so scared of being hurt that I could not get close to people.

The way I learned to cope with that fear and anxiety was to escape into religion. I spent a lot of time in church because the church was the center of our community. Even though my parents did not go to church, my sister and I attended the local Catholic elementary school, which was focused on religion and religious training, and there were a lot of services we went to during the week. I was not a good student because I had such a short attention span. But I decided when I finished grade school that I wanted to enter religious life of some kind to be trained as a priest or religious. That seemed to please my parents and my relatives, who always thought that I should enter religious life. I was happy that they were pleased so I applied to several seminary preparatory schools and chose the one, staffed by priests, furthest away from home in Indiana. It was on a lake and I liked it there. I did well in my studies but my spiritual life was based on guilt.

The second year I was there I came home for Thanksgiving. Holidays were occasion for festive family meals. My mother thought I was ill because I had grown so fast and so tall. She wanted me to stay home and go to the local public high school. It was during this period that I had my first drink. I was staying at a friend's house and during the middle of the night I couldn't sleep, so I found their liquor cabinet and helped myself to their bottle of vodka. I woke up the next day on their dining room floor. I had passed out and was full of shame and remorse when they found me there. But I had found the escape I had always wanted and never forgot that feeling of relief from anxiety and fear that first drink brought me.

I decided to return to the seminary in my senior year of high school. I entered a semi-cloistered monastery to consider a monastic vocation. There I completed my high school studies. When asked what I wanted to choose as my special assignment, I chose the sacristy so I could be close to the altar and the preparation for the Mass. The wine that was used for the Mass was made there and there was always a large supply kept in a separate room. So I began to sneak the wine. It helped me overcome my fears and anxiety so that I didn't have to care about anything. No longer would I have to be concerned that the powerful emotions that I felt inside would overwhelm me. I didn't drink on a daily basis but the remorse and guilt caused me to drink more. One of the monks was being treated for a spastic stomach with tranquilizers. So I wanted his medication too. Even though the doctor said I had a nervous stomach, he wouldn't give me any medication and I resented him for that.

Then I began to drink on a daily basis. I was not completing my college classroom assignments and my behavior changed. I became paranoid, feeling that everyone was watching me. I was reprimanded and warned about my drinking. One community picnic where there was a truckload of beer, I drank until I went into a blackout. The next day I was called into the prefect's office and asked to leave. I was told during a confrontation conducted by my superiors that the community would be better off without me. Apparently I had really made a fool of myself when I had blacked out. I was told that if I would leave there would be no black mark against my name. This statement, I know now, reflects the attitude of the community at that time concerning alcoholism. It was considered a moral issue and a weakness of character. The community was set up as a caste system with the older professed members ranking in authority and privileges. The alcoholic priests who were working in parishes were relieved of their ministries, recalled to the monastery, and then kept in isolation. It was a shame-based system of recovery. If you challenged the system at all you were kicked out. Meanwhile, a lot of enabling went on. The whiskey flowed freely at the social hour for priests and beer was provided for the brothers.

When I told my family that I was coming back home, I didn't tell them the truth. I was too ashamed. Instead, I told them that my nerves were bad, that everyone was picking on me, that I was overworked and overburdened. By then I was a functioning alcoholic. I just did what I had to do to get by. I became trained as a teacher, even though I didn't like teaching, because that was what I needed to do to be part of the community. I got out of teaching ministry because I didn't like it and went into parish work because there I could really get some drinking where no one could watch me. I was transferred by the church from place to place because of my drinking and poor attitude. Yet during this time I obtained two associate degrees, even with barely passing grades and the poor attendance due to my drinking.

When I finally came back home after many jobs in parish ministry, my parents had been separated, my sister was married, and I went to live with my mother. She began to see the way I drank. I had a few dollars saved but I needed to get into some kind of work. I couldn't let anyone know my background as a professed religious because of my shame. I took a job as a waiter, and I worked in restaurants and hotels where there was easy access to alcohol. I made enough money to get by. I drank on the job and at home, hiding bottles and isolating myself. By this time I had lost all spirituality. All I had left was religious guilt. I was ashamed to go to church because of what I looked like and smelled like. My mother was so disgusted with me that she threw me out. I went and got an apartment of my own. All I cared about was making enough money to pay my bills and keep myself supplied in booze.

I had my first hospitalization at the age of twenty-nine. I was a dumb drunk. I didn't know anything about withdrawal. I knew I was an alcoholic but would not accept that I had to do something about it. By not thinking about it my drinking would go away and I could control it. By now I was drinking up to a quart of vodka a day, at least. I was into maintenance drinking. I functioned as a robot. I was experiencing severe withdrawal symptoms and had to pass out to sleep and wake up with shakes and sweats and a thousand monkeys in my head and I needed another drink.

By the grace of God, when I went into grand mal seizures and DTs the nurse who lived next door to my apartment got me into the emergency room at the local hospital. They resuscitated me and called my family. I was in the hospital for three months with severe liver damage and an erratic heartbeat from withdrawal. Two specialists told me that if I took another drink I wouldn't live longer than a year. I had no insurance so medical assistance picked up the bill. I refused to sign for a liver biopsy and the doctor stated that other people wanted help, so why should he waste his time on me. I was enabled in that hospital. My friends that I worked with, my drinking buddies, sneaked in pints of vodka while I was in the hospital. The day I was released a woman doctor gave me some Antabuse and told me how important it was to get to AA meetings. But I was planning to drink again, so when she walked out of the room, I threw the pills away, left the hospital, and went to the nearest bar and ordered a double shot of vodka.

From then on I tried to control my drinking. I attended an AA meeting. The people were nice and friendly and I saw their serenity, but I also knew that they had to give up drinking to get that serenity. I continued to drink, switching to beer, trying to cut down, but it didn't work. I always went back to the vodka or whiskey. But my drink of choice was vodka. I bought the cheapest and put it in plastic jars. I needed it for the shakes, just to function. Meanwhile, my family and friends were concerned and would tell me about my drinking. I tried a counselor to get them off my back. He took me to a meeting and suggested an in-patient treatment center.

It was January. I was coming out of a bar. I had just bought a six-pack to get me through the night. It was cold and I slipped and fell and fractured my arm. They took me to the emergency room to be operated on. Coming out of the anesthesia, I went into another grand mal seizure and almost died as a direct result of lying about the amount I drank. I couldn't work but I continued to drink. I continued to have blackouts. I was detoxed four times.

Through the grace of God my bottom finally came at a time when I had stopped going to work. The only time I left the apartment was to get booze. My well-meaning friends had been supplying me with Valium. I had tried to detox myself with Valium and vodka for a year, in place of the booze. By now I was dully addicted. One day I had accumulated enough phenobarbital and muscle relaxers to take my own life, or so I thought. I took a handful of the pills and all the vodka and lay down on the bed to die. I remember planning to take the Clorox under the sink if that didn't work. Meanwhile, a priest friend of mine, who was a recovering alcoholic, was concerned about me. He had been praying for me but had not been able to get through to me. When I woke up, for a moment, I saw reality. I realized that God had a plan for me. He wanted me to live for some reason. I was scared to death but I was willing to take the chance and picked up the phone and called my priest friend.

He took me to detox and from there I went into a twenty-eight-day rehabilitation program.

The recovery process wasn't easy. It was the hardest thing that I had ever had to do in my life. I didn't sleep and had severe withdrawal for one year. My anxiety level was high and my blood pressure was up and then down. But my therapist gave me hope. She gave me hope that I was worth saving. From there I received the courage and strength to leave and go back to my old job, even though it was suggested that I not work, at least not at my old job. I asked the priest friend of mine to be my temporary sponsor. I went to meetings every day. I found a new sponsor who is still my sponsor today. My first year I functioned. All I could do was go to meetings and go to work, calling my sponsor and following what he told me to do. I couldn't drive a car for six months because I was an emotional basket-case. It was slow, difficult, and painful. But my Higher Power helped me through the pain, and I began to feel better about myself. I decided that I needed to go into a helping career. I was hired as a mental health counselor in a transitional home-care program. I began to change my thinking. Life became simpler. I worked the steps, completing my fourth and fifth step in my second year of sobriety.

After that I thought of my vocation again. I realized that I had been seeking God's approval. Now my concept of my Higher Power is Jesus Christ. He is loving and faithful. He is my Friend, my Father, and my Brother. I know that he forgives and he forgets. The more I have come to learn and the more I experience, the more I see part of God's plan for me. I become very emotional when I think of all the rewards I have received through my sobriety. Through the grace of God I have renewed my vocation and I'm now part of a community of brothers whose ministry is to serve God's people. I've made a lifetime confession of poverty, chastity, and obedience in order to be more available to hear and discern what the Holy Spirit is telling me. I have many significant people in my life today to enhance my spirituality and to keep me focused and to remind me by gentle nudges to get back on the path that God is leading me on.

I find that all the answers to my spirituality are in the Big Book. I'm attracted to the spirituality of the Desert Fathers, the monks of Mt. Athos, and the Jesus Prayer in its simplicity and selflessness. The spirituality in the Big Book is the same. It expresses the simple faith of simple men and women who have turned their lives over to the care of God as they understand him, and he has given them and given me the privilege of being part of the program of AA The church is beginning to change its way of treating alcoholics, to help them get into recovery instead of shaming and enabling them.

Today I want to live. God has given me back my life and a way to live one day at a time. I remember not so long ago waking up saying, "Another day, God, do I have to live another day?" Yet today I look at a fearful situation as a chance to grow. I still have many character defects to work on. Knowing that I am willing to do that is a miracle. The rewards that I have gained in my sobriety are many. I am filled with awe at the people God puts in our lives to help us grow and learn. Thank God for this singular grace for sobriety. Without the program there would not be sobriety and I would not be here.

5

NOURISHMENT

Good Soil: Friendly Churches

> God chose what is foolish in the world to shame the wise. God chose what is weak in the world to shame the strong....
>
> — 1 Corinthians 1:27

This was the passage of scripture chosen by Dr. Shoemaker for a pamphlet published by the Diocese of Maryland's Committee on Alcoholism entitled *What the Church Has to Learn from Alcoholics Anonymous.* In his book *Who Needs God?* Harold Kushner states that we reenforce our feeling of powerlessness or weakness by giving into temptation. Each time we give in to temptation we keep telling ourselves how weak we are.[1] Every time an addict gives in to the temptation to take a drink, use a mood-altering drug, or eat food compulsively it reenforces that sense of being out of control. To family members and friends it seems like foolishness to keeping doing what is so self-destructive. But God chose these "fools" to show the rest of the world what he expects of all of us.

It was Sunday morning and Marie was lonely. The big gray church building across the street with the red door looked cold to her. She leafed through her twelve-step meeting lists and found an Al-Anon meeting that met at noon at the Friends' meeting house down the street. She decided to go there because she knew she would find the friendship and comfort she needed. It was the same for Tony. He chose to spend the weekend at a Roman Catholic retreat center nearby. It was being sponsored by the local AA service board. There he knew he could grow spiritually and in fellowship with others overcome the temptation to drink again.

Dr. Shoemaker, being one of the first clergy to recognize that small group sharing could provide a way for addicts to resist temptation, opened up the hall at Calvary Church in New York City for one of the early Alcoholics Anonymous groups to meet. But they were encouraged to attend church services as well. Groups of recovering alcoholics and their spouses had been meeting during the week in homes and in tailor shops. As others joined they had to find a larger space. First it was Steinway Hall, then the Artists and Illustrators Club on West 24th Street. But they found that managing a club was a business enterprise and that helping drunks stay sober was what they were all about, not running a business. As the number of AA groups grew there was a need for some kind of organization, but the accumulation of wealth, property, and bureaucracy was a danger to be avoided. Meetings in church halls or buildings where rent could be paid for the space avoided these pitfalls. Now in almost every major city, churches have opened their doors for twelve-step meetings during the week. It is the good soil that keeps the program grounded in the love of the Body of Christ.

Water, Coffee, et al.

> Blessed is the man who trusts in the Lord. He is like a tree planted by the waters that sends out its roots by the stream and does not fear when heat comes, for its leaves remain green.
>
> —Jeremiah 17:7–8 RSV

Along the road by the Dead Sea, south of Jerusalem, are experimental projects to find ways to desalinate the sea and irrigate the desert. Now one sees patches of green in formerly dry places, where young seedlings can put their roots down into fresh water. Fresh water is important to the root system of any tree. So it is with human beings who also need refreshment. Alcoholics have sought that nourishment in alcoholic beverages. But alcoholic brews, even beer, provide a false sense of nourishment. In fact, beer-alcoholics become malnourished from lack of a nutritional diet when they rely only on this kind of sugar and carbohydrate diet.

At first, in the early stages of recovery, sugary foods and caffeinated beverages, such as coffee and tea, become a substitute for alcohol. When Bill W. and Dr. Bob first met in Henrietta Seiberling's home, they met in the kitchen where there was easy access to coffee, cake, and cookies, as well as talk. That tradition of coffee and cookies or cakes has carried over to all twelve-step meetings. Going early to set up the coffee pot and other refreshments is part of the chairman's job. It would appear that those predisposed to addiction seek more intense stimulation than others. However, it is questionable that caffeinated beverages and sweet snacks are the appropriate nourishments for addicts who have basic nutritional deficits and inadequate metabolic functions. Perhaps alternatives such as decaffeinated coffee and tea and vegetable and fruit snacks might be a better substitute.

But the refreshment time meets another need, that is, for social interaction both before and after the meeting. It is usual to see groups from a meeting sitting at a local restaurant to continue the discussion over yet another cup of coffee and to find help in dealing with personal issues. After years of isolated drinking, drugging, or eating, they are starving for intimacy. Those who did their drinking in a bar or cocktail party find meeting people with a liquid refreshment in hand a comfortable way of overcoming shyness, inherent in all addicts' personalities. This process helps to build up trust in one another and to break down denial.

Jesus Christ meets us over refreshments too, in a meal of thanksgiving and remembrance, called the Holy Communion or the Eucharist. He is always ready and eager to be in communion with us.[2] He comes to us to provide nourishment, food for our souls. He is present in the fellowship of the program of twelve-step recovery. The only criterion for membership is willingness to reach out and take the nourishment that is offered through the fellowship in the program.

Protection from Bugs: Nonalignment with Any Sect or Denomination

> Jesus was walking through some wheat fields on a Sabbath. His disciples were hungry, so they began to pick heads of wheat and eat the grain. When the Pharisees saw this, they said to Jesus, "Look, it is against our Law for your disciples to do this on the Sabbath."
>
> — Matthew 12:1–2 GNB

Jesus' feeding people on the Sabbath broke a rule that had grown up around the Torah, the Jewish Law, in order to feed people. He went on to remind the Pharisees that God wants kindness and compassion (Mark 3:4).

Traditions of Alcoholics Anonymous and Al-Anon have evolved because these recovering addicts and their family members believed that if they were to be able to help each other they needed to stay autonomous (tradition four) and self-supporting (tradition seven). The following story is shared in Al-Anon meetings:

> A group secured a meeting place in a church building. They offered to pay a small rental for the use of the room, but the minister said he was glad to let such a worthy society use it free of charge. But at every meeting the minister gave a long religious talk.
>
> The group couldn't object because of his generosity in giving them the use of the room. Many members were so confused by these sermons that they didn't come back a second time. The purpose of the group was lost. Finally it moved to quarters where they paid rent.[3]

For this reason, contributions are taken at twelve-step meetings to help defray the cost of renting church space to hold meetings. Bill W. tells the story of how someone died and left ten thousand dollars to the Alcoholic Anonymous Foundation in 1948. In the debate that ensued about taking the money, the foundation deliberately decided to stay poor and declined the outside contribution. The church might learn a lesson from the Alcoholics Anonymous Foundation! How often does a church accept money bequeathed in someone's will only to find that the will also contains a controlling clause, e.g., that the church must celebrate the Eucharist daily, or that the church must pay off its mortgage. Well-meaning people tie strings to the money they give. Well-meaning clergy tie strings to groups they allow to use their buildings for meetings. The nondenominational, autonomous nature of the "A" groups protects them and keeps them free to provide the services of feeding and freeing people in need.

Clean Air: Breath of New Life

> Then the Lord God took some soil from the ground and formed a man out of it; he breathed life-giving breath into his nostrils and

> the man began to live. Then the Lord God planted a garden in Eden, in the East, and there he put the man he had formed.
>
> — Genesis 2:7 GNB

Breath is the very substance of life. When we die we stop breathing. Breath is used in mouth-to-mouth resuscitation to revive someone who has stopped breathing. We know that life in the natural world is sustained by clean air, and when air pollution is high, trees and plants have a difficult time breathing.

The same is true for human beings. Dave Else describes an alcoholic or an addict as follows:

A human being;
A human being with a disease;
A human being with a disease that is chronic, progressive and potentially fatal;
A human being who probably inherited his/her predisposition to alcoholism/addictions;
A human being who has looked for the right things in the wrong places;
A human being who cannot see the truth of the disease because the disease creates a delusion state called denial;
A human being who needs compassion, understanding and, most of all, treatment;
A human being who has the potential for healing within but needs help and support to find it and to make it happen;
A human being who has much to offer others but who lacks belief in self;
A human being who lives with constant guilt, shame, and fear but cannot really express those feelings honestly;
A human being who is aided more in denial than in seeking help;
A human being who desperately wants a relationship with God and other human beings but feels unworthy of these;
A human being who sees all sorts of problems which cause him/her largely the consequences of alcohol/or other drugs;
A human being who needs our help to find the way into recovery and our support while in recovery;
A human being not much different from you and me![4]

It has been over fifty years since the beginning of Alcoholics Anonymous and the twelve steps. Yet much alcoholism and drug abuse have remained untreated even though treatment works.[5] The conservative figure is that one in ten alcoholics seek treatment, and of that one in ten only 10 percent are in long-time recovery. It is a sobering statistic. For every one alcoholic or drug addict, four others in the immediate family suffer the effects. Now we see massive problems of children of alcoholics and those who suffer from eating disorders because of parental addiction.

As a family counselor, I see the addiction disease played out in relationships. Subtle battles of control, blame, projection, anger, and escalating violence. The addiction, whether it be to alcohol, another drug, food, a long-held grievance, or each other is never talked about directly. The focus is often on what is said or what is done. Guilt and shame intensify as the person and/or the family stay enslaved by *addiction*. Tragically, family and marriage counselors do not understand the subtle dynamics of the addiction process and get caught up in it. The family disease of alcoholism is called the "merry-go-round of denial" or the "dance of anger." Often, the counselor gets on the merry-go-round and dances with the games being played out in the family or between the couple. The questions of chemical abuse — what, how much, how often, and when — are never asked of the clients. But naming the disease and naming its symptoms are vital to recovery and freedom.

It seems that we have just touched the tip of the iceberg in dealing with the addictive process and the multigenerational nature of addiction. We are learning that as one addiction is treated, others surface, so that the whole addictive process needs to be treated. Yet we are spending nationally more money for law enforcement than for treatment.

The first twelve-steppers recovered from their alcohol addiction in AA meetings, but many went on to suffer and die from complications of abuse of another addictive drug — nicotine. One rarely finds clean air to breathe at AA and NA meetings. Instead cigarette smoke fills the air. Today a few treatment centers are recognizing the need for addicts to be "substance free" and are treating nicotine addiction along with the alcohol and other drug addiction. There are now a few nonsmoking AA and NA groups and some Nicotine Anonymous meetings, based on the twelve steps. Nicotine addiction, like heroin addiction, is difficult to treat. Many recovering alcoholics are still in bondage to nicotine.

Addiction of any kind takes away freedom and destroys our ability to breathe easily. It is pollution of the worst kind because of its destruction of the human spirit. It is not just the social issue of the late twentieth century; it is a theological disease. For it is the freedom of the human spirit that God wants for each one of us, the freedom that he gave us in the Garden of Eden. But Adam and Eve wanted more than what God wanted for them. We, like them, are caught up in our own pride and willfulness and eventually become enslaved by our wrong choices, bonded to shame and to addiction. How often do we prefer to stay blind to our need and to the gift of the freedom of the twelve-step way to recovery! Yet God continues to provide opportunities to be free.

How refreshing it is to hear a counselor say to a couple or a family or to overhear in an Al-Anon family group, "You are powerless over alcohol (or another drug or food). Your life has become unmanageable. You didn't cause it, you cannot cure it, and you cannot control it. But you can recover from it."

How refreshing, how cleansing, how empowering!

Sunlight: The Slogans

> Here are proverbs that will help you recognize wisdom and good advice, and understand sayings with deep meaning. They can teach you how to live intelligently and how to be honest, just, and fair. They can make an inexperienced person clever and teach young men how to be resourceful. These proverbs can even add to the knowledge of wise men and give guidance to the educated, so that they can understand the hidden meanings of proverbs and the problems that wise men raise.
>
> — Proverbs 1:2–6 GNB

So it was with the wisdom literature in the Old Testament, particularly the moral and religious teachings in the Book of Proverbs. Included in these teachings is some very practical and common sense advice on how to live with one another. So it is also with the slogans found in every "A" meeting. Prominently displayed on the tables or on the walls of the meeting room, they are easy to read and to remember. They also help explain the steps to newcomers.

"Let Go and Let God"

Many books have been written about this slogan. It captures the essence of the first three steps, which are surrender, give in to God, and do it God's way.

Addicts and co-addicts are compulsive people. They want it done their way, on their timetable, and without regard to anyone else's wishes. But this slogan implies standing aside, submitting, then waiting, accepting, and receiving. It implies that we need to get out of God's way for God's will to be done, to stand under God's authority. In fact a paraphrase of "God as I understand him," might be better defined as "God as I stand under him."

Mary had been such a compulsive, take-charge person. She had grown up as the oldest child in an alcoholic family. She had learned to survive by taking charge of herself and everyone else in the family when her parents were not available because of their addiction. She became that way with her own family as well and was well known in the community because, if anyone wanted a task done, Mary was the person for the job. But she didn't make friends very easily. She was a tyrant at home and a slave driver to those who worked with her. It wasn't until her husband got into recovery from his alcoholism and she saw this slogan at her first Al-Anon meeting that her life began to change and she could begin her own recovery process from the disease of alcoholism.

> How great is God — beyond our understanding!
> The number of his years is past finding out.
> (Job 36:26)

"Easy Does It"

Another characteristic of an addict or a co-addict is a short fuse. It is so easy to react and escalate an argument, particularly because addicts love to put the blame in someone else's corner and to be defensive of themselves. Anger is carried on from one generation to another and builds with each succeeding generation.

Still another tendency is to rush in and save others like oneself. Bill W. tried to do this with the drunks at Calvary Mission, but he failed. Others of us have tried to save family members and friends and have also failed. We have learned the hard way about "Easy Does It" and "Live and Let

Live"! We learn, as others have, that the twelve-step way is to be servants and not bosses of others.

A question to ask when we feel these urges to respond or to try to save others is, "How important is it?" or "Why do I need to react or to be defensive when someone says or does something that is hurtful or derogatory? Isn't it more important to maintain my own health and serenity?" A rule to adopt might be the following:

> *Stop* and take a deep
> *Breath*, then silently
> *Measure* the feelings of anger and resentment, saying to oneself, "On a scale of one to ten can I measure my anger?" Then
> *Decide* what to do with the anger or resentment. Ask yourself, "Is it safe to tell the other person how what he or she has said or done makes me feel?" or "If it isn't, then can I physically work out my anger or aggressive instinct? Can I write about it or tell someone else or is it best just to ignore it and go on about my own business?"

It is important to remember that God judges our ways of responding or reacting as well as the other person's.

> For a Man's wants are in full view of the Lord, and he examines all his paths. (Prov. 5:21 NIV)

Saying the following prayer is another option:

> Most merciful Father,
> I confess that I have become insane again.
> I have allowed others to push my buttons.
> I have reacted instead of staying calm.
> I have focused on what others have said and done for me.
> I am truly sorry and I humbly repent.
> For the sake of your Son Jesus Christ,
> Have mercy on me and forgive me;
> that I might delight in your will,
> and walk in your ways,
> to the glory of your Name.
> Amen.[6]

"Listen and Learn"

This is a very hard slogan for co-dependents, which most of us are who grew up in alcoholic families. So often we monologue instead of dialogue when we communicate, so that no one else can get a word in! "Diarrhea of the mouth" is one way to describe this tendency to be always talking and never listening. It indicates self-centeredness and self-consciousness. But it also may be an indication that the person doing the talking is in much pain. One advantage of attending speaker meetings is that we cannot talk until the speaker is finished. One might just learn something that would touch this pain! Our ideas are important, but God wants us to listen more and talk less.

> Now then my sons [daughters], listen to me; blessed are those who keep my ways. Listen to my instruction and be wise; do not ignore it. Blessed is the man who listens to me, watching daily at my doors, waiting at my doorway. (Prov. 8:32–34 NIV)

"One Day at a Time"

> I won't look back. God knows the fruitless efforts, the wasted hours, the sinning, the regrets. I'll leave them all with him, who blots the record and mercifully forgives and then forgets.
>
> I won't look forward. God sees all the future. The road that's short or long will lead me home and he will face with me every trial and bear with me the burdens that may come.
>
> I will look into the face of Jesus, for there my heart can rest, my fears are stilled, and there is joy and love and light for darkness and perfect peace and every joy, is fulfilled.[7]

In recovery it is only this day that matters. There is no point in worrying about tomorrow or fretting over the past.

"Keep It Simple"

Westerners have a tendency to make things more complicated for themselves. More material goods, better communication exchange, and greater use of the world's resources can make life better or make life worse. Sometimes the bombardment of information seems overwhelming. The refreshing part of the twelve-step recovery process is that it is so simple to grasp. It doesn't take a theologian or an intellectual to figure it out. The more intellectual we are the harder it is for us to grasp the essence of the recovery process. This slogan speaks for itself.

> If you find honey, eat just enough — too much of it and you will vomit. (Prov. 25:16 NIV)

6

THREATS

> On his way back to the city early next morning, Jesus was hungry. He saw a fig tree by the side of the road and went to it, but found nothing on it except leaves. So he said to the tree, "You will never again bear fruit!" At once the tree dried up. The disciples saw this and were astounded. "How did the fig tree dry up so quickly?" they asked.
>
> — Matthew 21:18–20 GNB

Jesus frequently used trees and plants in parables to illustrate how people need to act in the kingdom of heaven. In this instance, Jesus pointed out to his disciples the power of faith and prayer. In the Jewish thought of that day vines and fig trees represented personal security. The root and the fruit of the tree went together and represented wholeness. The vitality of the tree was evidenced by the growth of the leaves, the fruit, and the spreading branches. So it is now with the twelve-step programs. To the casual observer it is a live and healthy tree. The fastest-growing movement in this decade is the self-help group phenomenon based on the twelve steps of Alcoholics Anonymous. If we look more closely, we can see evidence that the tree is being threatened by forces outside and inside the tree. Those threats are fundamentalism and evangelistic zeal, rejection by the church and its leaders, the weakening of the concept of the Higher Power, New Age spirituality, changes in the format and the wording of the steps, and the medical-scientific solution to alcoholism and other drug addiction.

Fundamentalism and Evangelistic Zeal

> Jesus healed many who were sick with all kinds of diseases and drove out many demons.
>
> — Mark 1:34 GNB

Sin or Sickness? Which comes first? Is alcoholism a moral issue or is it a disease? The Pharisees in Jesus' day believed that sin meant breaking the moral and ritual law of the Torah. They equated sin with sickness and believed that someone who was sick was unclean and that only God could absolve sin. For Jesus it didn't matter — the important thing was to make people well. In Jesus' day any evidence of mental illness was identified with the demonic. In the scriptures there are many instances of Jesus "driving out the demons" and healing the sick.

Whenever anything else takes the place of God as our ultimate concern in life, then we are open to demonic forces. Instead of worshipping God, in addiction we worship the thing or object. But the living Lord Jesus can cast away those demons. The twelve-step process of recovery is a way to bring us back into the way of salvation.

Surely there must have been alcoholism in Jesus' day! The Book of Proverbs provides a very clear picture of an alcoholic's love affair with alcohol.

> Wine is a mocker and beer a brawler. (Prov. 20:1 NIV)
>
> He who loves pleasure will become poor;
> whoever loves wine and oil will never be rich. (Prov. 21:17 NIV).

> Who has woe? Who has sorrow?
> Who has strife? Who has complaints?
> Who has needless bruises?
> Who has bloodshot eyes?
> Those who linger over wine,
> who go to sample bowls of mixed wine.
> Do not gaze at wine when it is red,
> when it sparkles in the cup,
> when it goes down smoothly!
> In the end it bites like a snake
> and poisons like a viper.

Your eyes will see strange sights
and your mind imagine confusing things.
You will be like one sleeping on the high seas,
lying on top of the rigging.
"They hit me," you will say, "but I'm not hurt!
They beat me, but I don't feel it!
When will I wake up
so I can find another drink?"
(Prov. 23:29–35 NIV)

Even Noah got drunk when the flood was over! One wonders how many alcoholics Jesus healed by "driving out the demons" caused by their addiction. Certainly he knew the consequences of excessive drinking were abominable to his Father. Proverbs 6:17–19 describes that demonic behavior:

A proud look, a lying tongue,
hands that kill innocent people,
a mind that thinks up wicked plans,
feet that hurry to do evil,
a witness who tells one lie after another,
and a man who stirs up trouble among friends. (GNB)

Duane J. Gartland, the executive director of Light of Life Mission, states that addicts' actions are insane but they do not know it. "We open ourselves up to the demonic through addiction, because we begin to deceive ourselves."[1] For alcoholics or addicts the greatest sin they have to avoid, on a daily basis, is taking the first drink or mood-altering drug because they know what the consequences are.

Although alcoholism was defined by the American Medical Association as a disease in 1956, the debate still rages in the religious community about whether alcoholism is a sin or a disease. In 1968 and then again in 1969, the National Council of Churches Task Force on Alcohol Problems met to review the recently issued surgeon general's report on "Alcohol Problems." Positions ranged from advocating abstinence to the complete acceptance of responsible drinking.[2] In 1965, the Boston Interfaith Clergy Conference and the North Conway Institute began a series of interfaith workshops for clergy. Their consensus was that both abstinence and moderation had religious motives, but that sobriety had a virtue that they all recognized.[3] Today efforts to deal with the problems of alcohol and addiction continue on the part of the National Interfaith Network on Alcohol and Drugs.[4] Yet clergy have little if any training in prevention and treatment of alcoholism even though the majority of pastoral issues involve alcohol-related problems. At present there are at least five gradations of positions held within the religious community regarding the use of alcohol.

1. *The use of any alcohol is a sin.* According to this position King Alcohol is the culprit. Alcoholics become sick and need to take a pledge of abstinence to stay away from their "sinful sickness." During the colonial period of American history there was much drunkenness, even at church services, and it was considered to be a sin, so signing a pledge of abstinence was the solution. When the Methodist Church was established in 1766, the use or purchase of distilled liquors by church members was forbidden.[5]

That policy was changed in 1968. Methodists still affirm, however, that the practice of abstinence is "a wise witness to God's liberating and redeeming love for mankind."[6] The influence of the Methodist Church and the American Temperance League (formed in 1826) led to the Prohibition Era from 1869 to 1933. There are still many small fundamentalist sects that believe in abstinence. This position is being widely adopted by adult children of alcoholics concerned about genetic risk factors of developing alcoholism. Those who adopt this position believe that, for them, drinking any alcohol is a sin. Recovering alcoholics will say that taking that first drink or mood-altering drug is a sin.

2. *Alcoholism is a personal sin that leads to sickness because of the sin of abuse.* This view is widely held by Roman Catholic theologians. Drinking in moderation is all right, but excessive drinking is not. The questionable nature of this position lies in how one defines moderation, since how alcohol affects a person depends on weight, age, sex, and family background. The Catholic bishops have provided leadership in addressing the need for a pastoral response to families and individuals affected by addiction. In a recent document, they ask for "prayers and personal involvement in bringing the Gospel message of hope and love to the terrible challenge of chemical dependency" and for the "healing hand of Christ."[7]

3. *Drinking is morally acceptable, but there are etiological and genetic factors that cause the person to become an alcoholic.* Those who are genetically susceptible to alcoholism have an allergic reaction to alcohol

and a deficiency in the adrenal cortical hormones (i.e., serotonin). Many have underlying depressive tendencies. This view is held by Alcoholics Anonymous and the National Episcopal Church's Coalition on Alcohol and Drugs.[8]

4. *Wine is acceptable for religious ceremonies and family celebrations.* This is the position of the Lutheran and Episcopal churches as well as Judaism, both reformed and orthodox. Since biblical times wine has been considered a good gift of God's creation to be enjoyed but not used intemperately. Jesus' first miracle at the wedding at Cana in Galilee was to turn water into wine for the enjoyment of the wedding guests. In their position statements, these churches differentiate between use, abuse, and dependency, as do other Protestant denominations in their statements on "chemical health."

5. *Alcoholism is a social sickness.* Rampant alcoholism is a symptom of a society that puts its values in power, self-aggrandizement, and self-indulgence and is in danger of moral and political decay. When humankind loses its dependence on God, worldly values and other gods, the gods of addiction, take over. Sin and alcoholism feed on each other in a society alienated from God and God's moral law.[9]

Dis-ease is the opposite of ease. Ease, tranquility, and peace as well as the appropriate use of God's created gifts have always been God's will for us. But we are fallen creatures, tainted with original sin. God has given us free will and we want to do right but evil lies close at hand: "I see in my members another law at war with the law of my mind and making me captive to the law of sin which dwells in my members. Wretched man that I am!" (Rom. 7:21). It is that fallenness which leads to disease. In the disease of alcoholism, the person "under the influence" becomes "captive to the law of sin" and cannot stop doing evil things.

In traditional Roman Catholic theology there are seven deadly sins: pride, greed, lust, anger, envy, gluttony, and sloth. Donald Capps expands that list to eight, with his addition of melancholy.[10] There are stages to these vices: first disorder, then dysfunction, and finally disintegration. Dr. Herbert Fingerat, a national leader in the treatment of alcoholism, states that in the United States we suffer from the social disease of addiction at the dysfunction stage. Recovering addicts, who have been in this dysfunctional stage, must guard themselves against "stinking thinking," which can be a danger signal of a potential relapse. Dr. Abraham Twerski calls this kind of thinking "addictologia,"[11] the kind of thinking that is meaningless because it is contradictory. Recovering alcoholics need to be vigilant about their anger and resentment, gluttony, pride, envy, indifference, and greed to keep from drinking again. Philip Parham, an Episcopal priest, puts it this way, "At the heart of our humanity is our sin, our pride, our self-centered stubbornness."[12] Family members of alcoholics or addicts often have the same sin of pride and stubbornness, which blocks the way for family recovery. Even in recovery co-addicts or co-dependents have to guard against melancholy or despair, anger, indifference, and control of others. As a society, we can fall into "stinking thinking" too. We, as a nation, need to recover from our societal sin of blaming and overindulgence, which has led to our present state. We all need the healing grace of God every day.

The churches have long ministered to alcoholics. The Salvation Army has been one of the most successful. The Emmanuel movement, from 1906 to 1929, pioneered a psychoreligious clinic at an Episcopal Church in Boston. Led by Dr. Elwood Worchester, it was the first program to treat alcoholism without increasing the alcoholic's guilt.[13]

Some charismatic "born again" Christians, however, realizing that they forfeited their prerogatives for healing that come from Jesus Christ to the techno-scientific health care industry, are sending teams of renewed Christian lay and ordained ministers into the streets for laying on hands for healing. They also incorporate anointing with oil and laying on of hands into regular communion services. In this enthusiasm to reclaim the power of God for restoration to health and wholeness, it is important not to forget that, while deliverance and freedom can at times be given instantaneously through the supernatural intervention of the Holy Spirit, people who are addicted to alcohol or other drugs need help to maintain that deliverance. Because of the powerful nature of addiction, when "stinking thinking" gets out of hand or the next crisis comes in the life of healed persons, they are under severe pressure to return again to the drugs that they relied on to cope with pain, resentment, and disappointment before God moved in their lives. Even "born again" Spirit-filled Christians who abstain from alcohol can become addicted to prescription medication!

Many Christians from traditionally fundamentalist backgrounds still believe that if a person accepts Jesus Christ as Lord and Savior that alcoholism or drug addiction will be instantly healed or cured. Do they tempt God by assuming God will work through them for healing? Or do they manipulate God by saying God will heal if we just use the right eucharistic formula? Healing takes place for God's purposes and to manifest God's power; it also takes place because a person has faith and takes the appropriate steps needed for that healing to occur. Humility and a constant awareness of the omnipotence of God and our humanness are essential to guard against these presumptions.

Healing of addiction through the supernatural intervention of the Holy Spirit outside of twelve-step recovery programs is rare. Sometimes addicts tell of their urge to drink being miraculously taken away through a spiritual encounter with the living Lord Jesus. They may stay sober or clean for years. But addiction is a complex disease, involving nutrition, the emotions, the will, and the pleasure center of the brain.[14] Those vulnerable to alcoholism because of genetic and environmental influences need treatment. Genetic vulnerability plus alcohol leads to alcoholism and other related diseases. In other words, the weaknesses of the fathers and mothers pass on to the children.

Rejection by the Church and Its Leaders

The real sin of the church with regard to alcoholism and other addictions is its misinformation about the physiological aspects of the disease. George Pierce, the national director of the Church Army, stated in a recent newsletter that to treat alcoholism as an addiction is a form of "weak grace," that sin is the real culprit. His Church Army, like the Salvation Army, wants to bring addicts to Jesus Christ to be saved from their sin.[15]

But with the disease of addiction the physiological and emotional damage needs to receive healing as well as the spiritual damage. As we have seen, AA provides a sound theological and spiritual discipline for surrender to God, confession, repentance, reconciliation, and redemption, worked through on a daily basis. It is my experience, as an addictions counselor that lasting deliverance comes only with time, beginning with some form of detoxification and rehabilitation treatment, followed by a period of at least a year of regular counseling, along with attendance at support group meetings with a serious spiritual discipline. Pastors and other religious leaders who discount the need for these aspects of recovery do more harm than good. During the first year or two of sobriety, there is a real danger of relapse. An alcoholic or drug addict is always recovering and never cured. Well-meaning Christians are guilty of presumption when they say that alcoholics or addicts who have accepted Jesus Christ are saved and are therefore permanently cured. This conclusion is too often dispelled by a return to drinking or drugging after the conversion experience.

The story of Polly illustrates that accepting Jesus does not rescue one from the ravages of addiction. It also illustrates how in the name of Jesus addicts can be kept in bondage by others. At the age of twenty-four Polly, addicted to alcohol, food, sex, and abuse, has been in and out of women's shelters for the past ten years. She has been evangelized and hospitalized many times and has at each point of crisis accepted Jesus Christ. She was a victim of incest and sexual and physical abuse as a child and learned to cope with this abuse just as her mother, now dead, coped with the abuse of her father, who was a violent alcoholic. She claims she had twins by her father when she was thirteen. At fourteen her cousin introduced her to prostitution. Frequent sex with men is the only way she knows to get affection. She feels rotten inside and uses alcohol to cope with her feelings of worthlessness and rage. She has been evicted from shelters because of her violence when drinking. In spite of the many times she has accepted Jesus Christ, he seemingly has not rescued her from her addictions. Once she was "saved" by a "minister" who got her out of the church-sponsored shelter and into his "shelter," where he kept women in Bible study groups. While there she married a man, also staying in the shelter (which did not meet county health standards), who beat her to get her welfare checks. She wasn't permitted to go to Alcoholics Anonymous meetings, but was kept in abandoned homes, bought with food stamp monies, and told to be submissive in her Bible study classes.

To survive she periodically threatens suicide so that she can stay in a local hospital for a few nights and get some needed attention and relief. She has taken out numerous abuse warrants against her husband but each time has dropped charges and goes back to him and to the abuse. The last time she left her husband he had been jailed for rape of a minor. She returned to the streets on a drinking spree, lashing out at others and making sexual alliances with some of the homeless men she met there. When she checked herself into the hospital with her latest suicide attempt, she was covered with lice and sores and she now tested positive for HIV virus. She will find her salvation from her addictions when she dies.

When addicts have admitted their problem with alcohol or other drugs and surrendered to God, it is only a beginning of a life-long process. Like God's saving power, which is an ongoing process, so is recovery. Jesus told his disciples, "Go and bear fruit — fruit that will last" (John 15:16). As we have examined in earlier chapters, the fruit on the renewed tree of life is every recovering person working the steps in the program for a lifetime, "each tight little bud and leaf begins to open up as the entire plant turns to drink in the life-giving light of the Twelve Steps."[16]

There is a misconception among the Christian community that alcoholics can "control" their drinking. There is an old saying that once a man takes a drink the drink takes the man. Robert Godley, an Episcopal priest, puts it this way, "The consequences of [an addict's] choices accreted over a period of time eventually render subsequent choices progressively less free until they are nothing more than compulsive responses to addictive craving."[17] When the invisible line from abuse to dependency is crossed the person affected is powerlessness to control what happens. Will power is nonexistent. It is important for church members to be educated about the progression of the disease to understand that an addicted person does not have that option. Well-meaning religious people often intensify the guilt of addicts by chastising them for not "trying hard enough" to quit. It is the willingness to give up trying to control that is the turning point needed for the process of recovery to begin.

John Baudhuin, an Episcopal deacon who treats alcoholics, comments:

> Tragically, most human institutions lose touch with their purpose after a given time, and religions have certainly not been exempted from this problem. Some of us carry deep hurts from painful messages inflicted upon us by well-meaning people in various religious groups. It is important that we open up and share these hurts and then go on from there. Sometimes the hurts have been too great for any means of return. In other cases, we may be able to return. As always, this is an individual choice. A great irony in today's world is that of the recovering alcoholic returning to his childhood church not for forgiveness, but to forgive them![18]

Pastors who counsel those suffering from the disease of addiction can either enhance the restoration to freedom and faith or turn the addict farther away from that gift of God's grace and healing. Clergy must be trained to treat addiction and be sensitized to the hurt and pain underneath the apparent "sinful" and irresponsible behavior of the addicted person. It is important, also, for clergy and other religious leaders to be trained to counsel the family members to detach from the addicted person and to assist in the planning for an intervention under the direction of a professional. Rev. Godley adds that the sacrament of healing and reconciliation should be made available only at an appropriate time in the recovery process.

The following are guidelines for the religious community in helping addicts:

- Provide a semester course in clergy seminary training in addiction and intervention and require ongoing clergy refresher courses.
- Encourage twelve-step support groups in your church for members of your congregation and others.
- Educate members of your congregation in the roots and workings of the twelve steps.
- Encourage every layperson to attend one such group for six sessions.
- Invite a recovering addict or family member to give his or her lead as a sermon once or twice a year.[19]

Unless the religious community takes seriously this challenge to be educated and trained about addiction, the "war against drugs" will not be won. Instead, the twelve-step programs for recovery may die, just as the Washingtonians did, because of the rejection by the religious establishment.

Higher Power: Whatever I Want It to Be

Thou shalt have no other gods before me.

— Deuteronomy 5:6 RSV

"It doesn't matter what your Higher Power is, as long as it works to keep you sober. It could even be that light bulb over there." This concept of Higher Power was introduced at a recent AA meeting by the speaker for the evening.

Other concepts of the Higher Power abound in the literature; see for example the diagram on p. 117.[20]

	FORCE	QUALITY	LEVEL OF CONSCIOUSNESS	BASIC URGE	PITFALL	MASTERY
BEING	7th The Love of God (Self)	Self-Mastery	Love/Will (Being)	Unity	(Indiscriminate Use of Will)	Transformation
	6th The Love of Life	Intuition/ Altruism	Love/Wisdom (Higher Emotions)	Compassion	(Over-Identification with Humanity's Suffering)	Revelation
	5th The Love of Truth	Comprehension/ Authentic Expression	Active Intelligence (Higher Mind)	Understanding	(Abstraction)	Illumination
	4th Awakening	Harmonizing Higher with Lower Nature	Harmony Through Conflict	Acceptance Harmonizing	(Attachment To Conflict)	Self-Creation
BECOMING	3rd The Will to Know	Self-Definition	Analysis/Comparison (Concrete Mind)	Identity Seeking	(Fragmentation)	Right Thought
	2nd The Will to Feel	Self-Gratification	Pleasure/Devotion (Sensual/Emotional)	Passion	(Duality)	Right Feeling
	1st The Will to Live	Self-Preservation	Order (Physical/Instinctual)	Fear	(Isolation)	Right Action

Transpersonal Dimension (Out of Time)
7
6
5
Inner World of Wisdom
Domain of Essence
4
Personal Dimension (Time)
3
2
1
Outer World of Experience
Domain of Ego

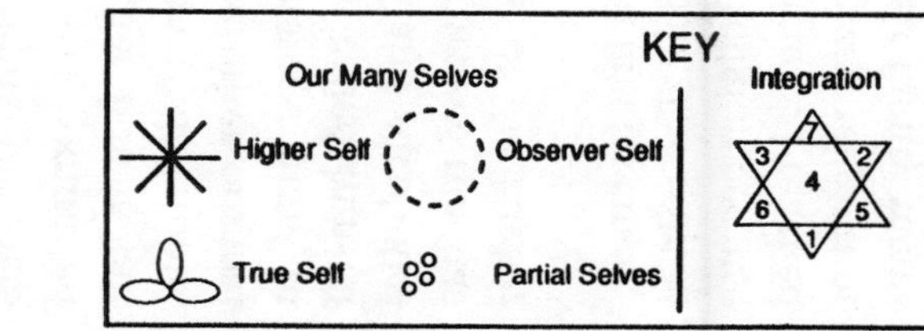

The psychologist who developed this model claims that the wisdom of AA is the same philosophy that is reflected in the universal consciousness of all organized religions, namely, that one can believe in a Higher Power and that life is worth living. Her theory is that the twelve-step programs reflect seven levels of consciousness as she has diagramed, each one leading to a higher level of being and becoming.

As we have seen, Bill Wilson's original concept of the Higher Power came out of his spiritual awakening through his involvement with the Oxford Group movement and his committing his life to Jesus Christ at the Calvary Church Mission. He received much feedback when he circulated his version of the twelve steps among the original founders of Alcoholics Anonymous. Some of the more religiously committed members favored the emphasis on God as the Higher Power, but others did not. Among the latter was a salesman from Philadelphia, the founder of AA in Philadelphia. He convinced the other original members of AA to use the phrase, "God, as we understood Him," in the third and eleventh steps of the twelve steps. He called himself a theological rebel.[21] Bill Wilson finally compromised and Alcoholics Anonymous accepted that concept. Over the years, however, this has led to a looseness in the program and a humanizing of the Higher Power.

It is important to recognize that many come into their first few meetings of AA, NA, Al-Anon, or ACOA as theological rebels. The pain of addiction is so great there is anger at God or organized religion because God or the church has not rescued me from my addiction. Preached at, cajoled, and judged by those who represent organized religion or a church denomination, recovering alcoholics and their family members can get violently angry when the name of Jesus is brought up because they have confused the institution of Christianity with Jesus of the Gospels. As defenses are softened and one finds acceptance and love from other sufferers in the fellowship of the program, rebelliousness gradually gives way. But this rebelliousness, or resistance to authority, is characteristic of the addict's dis-ease and requires pastoral sensitivity and patience on the part of the religious community.

But this was not the intent of the majority of the original founders of AA. Here are some of their words from *Alcoholics Anonymous:*

> I came into A.A. solely for the purpose of sobriety but it has been through A.A. that I have found God."

> I began to read the Bible daily and to go over a simple devotional exercise as a way to begin each day.
>
> I found a friend who never lets me down and is ever eager to help. I can actually take my problems to Him and He gives me comfort, peace and happiness.[22]

They had found a spiritual way to wholeness on the journey of their recovery from addiction. In the process of surrendering, accepting their powerlessness, taking a moral inventory, and making amends, they had experienced the power of God's grace acting in their lives. They had had a life-changing, spiritually transforming experience.

For thousands of years, men and women have been striving to find God, first enshrining him[23] in monuments of stone, then making images of themselves as gods. The First Commandment reminds us that God says, "Thou shall have no other gods but me." The Apostle Paul stood on the hill of Ares where the Court of Areopagus met in Athens almost two thousand years ago. Above him gleamed the Parthenon, the monument to the Greek deities made in the likeness of human beings. There he was asked to defend his "philosophy":

> I see that in every way you are very religious [spiritual]. . . . The God who made the world and everything in it is the Lord of heaven and earth and does not live in temples built by hands as if he needed anything. And he is not served by human hands, because he himself gives all men life and breath and everything else. From one man he made every nation of men, that they should inhabit the whole earth; and he determined the times set for them and the exact places where they should live. God did this so that men would seek him and perhaps reach out for him and find him, though he is not far from each one of us. For in him we live and move and have our being (Acts 17:22–28 NIV).

Paul might be saying to twelve-steppers everywhere today that the God who created and inspired the twelve steps is here for them to reach out and find him. The message is the same for everyone, in every age and culture. As the psalmist says in Psalm 18: "It is God who arms me with strength and makes my way perfect."

This same God gives addicts the strength to recover from their addictions. He is the One who calls for repentance, to turn away from the enslavement of addiction and to follow him. To build up ourselves or to enshrine "the Program" as the way to salvation comes dangerously close to "enshrining" the gift and not the giver. If the twelve steps work, they ought to keep us moving toward God and not away from him.

We have been given the liberty of finding this God through the process of *metanoia* and renewed life that the twelve steps provide. The Higher Power "of our understanding" gives us that freedom. God never coerces us to find him. The danger in that license is that we will remake God into reflections of ourselves, like the deities of Athens. Instead God made us in his image, to be perfected by him and not by ourselves. He receives us as "adopted sons and daughters" and we relate to him in our own uniqueness and specialness, as children to a loving parent. He came to earth as a human being, to become one of us so that we could be one with him. God is not an inanimate object, like a light bulb. He is a personal God whom we can call *Abba*, and he meets each one of us in a personal way. Although we need to hold ourselves accountable to God through spiritual guides and mentors and through our interactions with others, God is not the group consciousness, however important that is to maintaining our recovery from addictions.

The God from my understanding and from the understanding and witness of many other Christians who have gone before me is that the spiritual way is through God's Son, Jesus Christ. He speaks of himself as the Way, the Truth, and the Life (John 14:6). He is the only way to wholeness; and those who worship him must worship him in spirit and in truth.

The New Age Gnosticism: Spiritualism and Cosmic Humanism

> God is a Spirit, and those who worship him must worship in spirit and in truth.
>
> — John 4:24 NEB

> To be controlled by human nature results in death; to be controlled by the Spirit results in life and peace.
>
> — Romans 8:6 GNB

Enter many bookstores today and you will find a section marked "Self-help Books" or "Recovery Books, Magazines, and Tapes." The titles range from *Homecoming: Reclaiming Your Inner Child* (Bradshaw) and *Reflections on the Light* (Shakti Gawain) to *Journey into Shamanism with Woman Between the Wind* (Heather Hughes-Calero). The magazines are titled *East-West Journal, Changes, Women of Power,* and *Yoga Journal,* and *New Age Journal.* Circulation of the *New Age Journal* was 165,000 in 1989. There are now some 456 New Age publications. The tapes are for relaxation, imaging, and journeying inward. There are twelve-step workbooks and variations on the twelve steps for every conceivable cause and problem.

The New Age is here! It is the Age of Aquarius![24] Buddhist centers and feminist spirituality, crystal empowerment bags, earthy spirituality for an evolving planet are dangerously influencing the twelve-step movement, particularly the Adult Children of Alcoholics groups. Yet the New Age movement is not new. During the first four centuries of Christianity, such movements were then called Gnosticism, Manachaeism, and Pantheism and provoked the formation of the Nicene Creed. The early Christian Fathers defended the faith against the intrusion of these heretical doctrines on the fledgling Christian faith. Today's heresies are similar to these early heresies and are flourishing in our Western pluralistic society.

The New Age movement is a broad-based movement of people hungry for spirituality who are not being fed by organized religion. The movement emphasizes healing without reference to Christianity. New Agers represent 5 to 10 percent of the United States population and as much as 15 percent of those residing in Eastern and Western cities.[25] Ronald Enroth, in his book *Lure of the Cults,* describes the movement as psychospiritual, with an emphasis on inner experience and achievement of detached tranquility.[26] Ralph White, of New York's Open Center, describes it as "an enormous spectrum involving the body, mind and spirit, including an increased awareness of nutrition, the rise in ecological thinking, a change in business perspectives, a greater emphasis on the individual's intuition."[27] It has arisen partly out of the 1960s human potential movement and the rampant narcissism of the 1970s and 1980s. Its gospel is positive confession and the god within. Both John A. T. Robinson and Norman Vincent Peale have had an influence on the movement.[28] The language used includes "new kind of ministry," "healing the inner self," "I am working on my recovery," "journeying," "all is one," "all is god," and "finding the god within me."

Spiritualism, such as that found in Buddhist meditation, separates the spirit from the emotions and the body and was known in the early Christian church as a form of Gnosticism. Jack Kornfield, a meditation teacher and clinical psychologist in Woodacre, California, describes some "stunning spiritual experiences" in a Buddhist monastery in Thailand in the 1970s. But he found that he had the same fears when he returned to the United States. Vietnam veterans practicing meditation to overcome post-traumatic stress syndrome found that asking for forgiveness could do more for healing the pain than any amount of meditating![29]

There are limits to how much human beings can transform themselves or how much they can avoid facing the pain and suffering common to all of humankind. This new/old brand of attempting detachment and sereneness in the midst of suffering is only a way of avoiding or denying the reality of pain and suffering.

Yet contemplation and meditation have their place in seeking to be in communion with God, the transcendent Holy One, King of the Universe. The fourth-century Desert Fathers found those times in the wilderness refreshing and spiritually renewing. But they didn't stay in the wilderness; they came back to help others. So did Jesus. Although he felt it important to go off into the hills to pray and be with his Father in heaven, he came back to continue his ministry of preaching, teaching, and healing. For addicts the danger of too much time in contemplation and separation from others is that of relapse. Addictive cravings are subtle and real, and the addictive mind loves to play deceptive tricks even on the most spiritual of human beings. Only in community with other suffering and recovering human beings can an addict face the pain so that it can be dissipated.

It is noteworthy that although Buddhism rejects materialism, New Age spiritualism accepts it.[30] Martyrdom is frowned upon; it is "me first, you second." It is works-righteousness oriented. Often in twelve-step meetings one hears the following phrases: "You are not working your program," or "You need to go to more meetings." One gets the impression that there is something magic in recovery and that if one is not continually in the process of recovery one is somehow not "with it."

In the Judeo-Christian religion God accepts us and forgives us; God realized our fallenness and sent his son, Jesus Christ, to redeem us and give us his grace. God, in his infinite wisdom and understanding, realizes that no matter how hard we try we can never be good enough and that we can easily be tempted. He walked with humankind in the Garden of Eden and then protected man and woman when they disobeyed his command and ate of the tree of the knowledge of good and evil. He knew that humankind would always want to be like God and would next want to possess the tree of life and eat and live forever. But God said "for dust you are and to dust you will return" (Gen. 3:19b). He still walks with humankind in the gardens of temptation, protecting us from our weaknesses. Not only can humankind not achieve perfection; we cannot achieve morality or cleansing from sin, either by imaging ourselves that way or by healing the child within. For the hurting child within needs a Savior. The hurting child within needs to be forgiven and to forgive those who have done us wrong. The hurting child within can best be made whole through the Holy Spirit of the Triune God, the Incarnate One, the Risen Lord Jeshua, or Jesus. Even orthodox Judaism looks to *Hashem*, the King of the Universe, for salvation and not to some inner gods or human strivings.

The twelve steps were formed from Christian cell groups, where sharing one's Christian faith journey attracted others. Robert Bellah cites the need for this sense of community in *Habits of the Heart*.[31] Alcoholics Anonymous functions in the same way. But all the twelve-step groups do not function in the same way. The twelve-step movement is moving closer and closer to becoming a sect, which calls itself more authentic and real than the institutional church — and in many ways it is.

In their attempts to find drugless alternatives and natural highs, both spiritualism and cosmic humanism have appealed to those recovering from addiction. Meditation and relaxation techniques are alternative ways to find some inner peace, to help with the depression underlying much addiction. Our centuries-old mystic traditions within Roman Catholicism, such as the Desert Fathers experienced, have a lot to offer to these recovering addicts.

We have become a nation constantly doing or going, controlled by our wrist watches and our machines. God ordained a Sabbath day of rest for each of us. Jesus invited his disciples to "come away by yourselves to a lonely place, and rest awhile." For then, as today, they were always coming and going, worrying about tomorrow. Since the beginning of the twentieth century humankind has had little time for solitude. Noise of the radio or the television blots out our time with God. "Silence is golden" is wisdom to be regained from the sages; learning again to be quiet and rest helps still compulsivity and obsessiveness. Ericksonian hypnosis, or therapeutic relaxation, can help to heal smoking addiction. Finding ways to counter negative childhood messages is important in the recovery process from family abuse. But many in the recovery community are going off on the fringes and into what traditional Christianity has taught are heretical ways to seek recovery.

As cosmic humanism and spiritualism creep into the twelve-step movement, will the "A" groups become just another do-it-yourself American social phenomenon? The specific danger for those recovering from addiction is that the powerful temptations of greed, self-centeredness, pride, and control will take over, just as they did in the early days of the Washingtonians. Already one hears in the ACOA and co-dependency movements, "My bill of rights comes first." If we are always concerned about our rights, how can we be of service to others? If we are constantly seeking some elusive cosmic oneness, we will remain unfulfilled and unsatisfied. The original founders of Al-Anon learned to live with the disease of alcoholism one day at a time, just as their recovering alcoholic spouses did in AA. They found peace and happiness through working the steps of the program. Somehow God gave them the wisdom and strength to follow God's way, not their own. That doesn't mean that where there is physical, emotional, or sexual abuse in an alcoholic family that the recovering person shouldn't separate him- or herself to regain self-esteem and self-respect. Depending on the extent of the abuse, the willingness of the spouse to change, and the coping options available to the abused party, God's will is often separation.

Where is the institutional church as people by the hundreds and thousands flock to twelve-step groups? Morton Kelsey states that the theological rigidity of the established churches is directly responsible for preventing the intervention of God's grace in healing diseases.[32] Perhaps the "church" is becoming just another dysfunctional family system, keeping addicts and their family members from experiencing the real grace of God by perpetuating the blame and denial of the alcoholic family system. That is the way it appears to many in recovery from addiction. Looking for some kind of family connection, individuals recovering from their family disease of addiction are flocking to Adult Children of Alcoholics or co-dependency groups. They find in these twelve-step support groups a way to connect, to find fellowship and acceptance. Still seeking networking and some inner peace, they are easily attracted to the fringe: spiritism, shamanism, and cosmic humanism. Kelsey says that this will continue as long as the "church" prevents the continuing action of God's healing power to be available to people who are hurting.

Changes in the Format and the Wording of the Steps

In the sphere of earth we lose all we love; in the sphere of heaven we find all we lose.

— Father Andrew, Anglican Fellowship of Prayer

Along with the New Age movement has come a broad-based revision of the steps to suit the needs of various causes, for example, the environmental movement and feminism; Alcoholics Anonymous World Service office has a specific format to be used in changing the wording of the steps. Many groups have altered that wording while referring to their own version as the twelve steps.

It was Earth Day revisited and environmental awareness was in the air. The Greenpeace spirit and the spirit of the twelve-step movement had come together and a new organization was born: the Greenspirit Center of Manchester, New Hampshire. "I am yours in the greening Mystery that trembles throughout the universe," says its founder, Albert J. LaChance.[33] Greenspirit calls itself an organization of men and women who have accepted personal responsibility for the fate of Mother Earth and have adopted the twelve steps to provide a path to help them change the dysfunctional behaviors within all life systems. These are the steps they have adopted:

1. We admit that we are powerless over an addicted society, that our lives and all of life have become degraded.

2. We come to acknowledge the existence of an Originating Mystery accomplishing the evolution of the universe; and accept that, if allowed, this Originating Mystery will reveal to each of us our natural relationships to self, to others, to other species, to the earth and to the universe.

3. We decide to surrender our lives and our wills to this Originating Mystery, however we chose to name it.

4. We examine ourselves, listing all our attitudes and actions that damage the created order, thereby stopping or impeding the emergence of the Originating Mystery.

5. We acknowledge to ourselves, to the Originating Mystery and to another person the specifics of our deluded thinking, attitudes and behavior.

6. We become entirely willing to have all habits of delusion removed from our thought, our attitudes and from our behavior.

7. In humility we request that this Originating Mystery remove all our habits of deluded thought, attitude and behavior.

8. We make a list of all persons, all other species, and all the life systems of the planet we have harmed; and become ready to do everything in our power to heal them.

9. We make a strenuous effort to heal all phases of the created order, human, animal or planetary, injured by our deluded thinking, attitudes or actions.

10. We continue on a daily basis to go on examining our thinking and our actions as to whether they foster or impede the emergence of life. Where they impede this emergence we admit it and change.

11. We continue through physical-mental-spiritual disciplines to so change ourselves as to improve our own ability to foster the emergence and health of the whole created order.

12. Having experienced a re-awakening to self, to humanity, to all species, to the planet and to the universe, we try to spread this awareness to others and to practice these disciplines in all phases of our lives.

Defining their cause as befriending the Earth and befriending the Universe, or the New Catholic Mysticism, Carol and Albert LaChance are among many who are revising the twelve steps to suit a personal cause.

Another movement changing the steps to suit its needs is a group of recovering alcoholic women. Finding that the original twelve steps were primarily influenced by recovering men alcoholics and that women have special needs and issues in recovery different from men, Gail Unterberger has redesigned the steps as follows:

1. We have a drinking problem that once had us.
2. We realized that we needed to turn to others for help.
3. We turn to our community of sisters and our spiritual resources to validate ourselves as worthwhile people, capable of creativity, care and responsibility.
4. We have taken a hard look at our patriarchal society and acknowledge those ways in which we have participated in our own oppression, particularly the ways we have devalued or escaped from our own feelings and needs for community and affirmation.
5. We realize that our high expectations for ourselves have led us either to avoid responsibility and/or to overinvest ourselves in others' needs. We ask our sisters to help us discern how and when this happens.
6. Life can be wondrous or ordinary, enjoyable or traumatic, danced with or fought with, and survived. In our community we seek to live in the present with its wonder and hope.
7. The more we value ourselves, the more we can trust others and accept how that helps us. We are discerning and caring.
8. We affirm our gifts and strengths and acknowledge our weaknesses. We are especially aware of those who depend on us and of our influence on them.
9. We will discuss our illness with our children, family, friends and colleagues. We will make it clear to them (particularly our children) that what our alcoholism caused in the past was not their fault.
10. As we are learning to trust our feelings and perceptions, we will continue to check them carefully with our community, which we will ask to help us discern the problems we may not yet be aware of. We celebrate our progress toward wholeness individually and in community.
11. Drawing upon the resources of our faith, we affirm our competence and confidence. We seek to follow through on our positive convictions with the support of our community and love of God.

12. Having had a spiritual awakening as a result of these steps, we are more able to draw upon the wisdom inherent in us, knowing we are competent women who have much to offer others.[34]

The twelve steps can be used by anyone, claims Joe Klaas, to achieve success and happiness, to improve life.[35] It naturally follows that the condition of the earth, the condition of the universe, and the condition of women can be improved as well, so anyone can revise the steps to suit a particular purpose and even add a new step. A new sexual abuse group in Pittsburgh has done just that. Notwithstanding the rightness of the cause, drastically changing the wording of the steps waters them down so that they lose their original substance.

Medical-Scientific Solution

Classifying alcoholism and other addictions as diseases is important in the recovery process and helps to break down the denial systems that addicts build up to protect themselves from facing their addiction. Going to a physician or a hospital to be treated for a disease is acceptable in our civilization. But Dr. Silkworth, Carl Gustav Jung, and William James all taught the early founders of Alcoholics Anonymous that alcoholism was more than just a physical illness. "The best cure for dipsomania [another term for alcoholism]," said William James" is religiomania."[36]

It is ironic that we in the United States are moving away from the spiritual basis and the original intent of the twelve-step recovery process while those who specialize in treating alcoholism in the Soviet Union are excited about the spirituality of the twelve-step support groups. The Soviet way of treating alcoholism through science and psychiatry, divorced from any ties to organized religion or the twelve-step process, has been a dismal failure.

Fortunately, in the United States our alcoholism and other addiction treatment centers have found that the twelve-step process to recovery works best. These treatment centers are giving new hope to addicts and their family members. Unfortunately, they are now falling under the same restraints as the rest of the health care industry, subject to the mandates of the insurance companies, the dictates of the government, and the whims of the managed care industry. The economics of managed care are important for large corporations, which have experienced a 47 percent increase in health care costs. But managed care has become "rationed care."[37] As we learn more and more about the physiology of addiction and as disorders associated with addiction recovery become more complex, we have the worst conditions for treating the disease.[38] The length of the hospital stay and the type of treatment, including the interpretation of the spirituality of the twelve-step programs and whether that treatment is in-patient or out-patient, are now being determined by these forces.

As those who treat addictions become "professionals" with licensing and certification, the treatment of alcoholism and other addictions will move away from God's intent for recovery, which is through the twelve steps and people helping people, without pay. It has "worked" without government, professionalism, or the insurance industry. Someone once suggested that Bill W. turn professional, but he would not take a penny for doing twelve-step work. Even though addiction has become more complex today than it was when AA was founded, people can get better through the twelve-step programs. Professional counselors and physicians can enhance the process of recovery if they recognize that central to the healing process is spiritual health.

Scientists studying alcoholism and its genetic markers say they are close to a breakthrough and have been for ten years. Soon, they tell us, they will be able to identify those markers. We know that the genetic risk of developing alcoholism or another addictive disease is 50 percent higher for those who come from chemically dependent families, estimated to be one American in four. But this does not keep individuals from those families from using mood-altering drugs. "I see in my members another law of sin which dwells in my members" (Rom. 7:23), stated St. Paul, and so the disease of alcoholism will never be cured, not even by our scientific advances, as important as they are.

Christians who believe that alcoholism is a sin and the medical, technical, and scientific community, which classifies addiction as a neuroallergic disease, need to learn from each other. For in the disease of alcoholism and addiction sin and sickness go together. Both need to be addressed in recovery. Recovery is a spiritual process as well as a medical one. Gerald May writes, "Humanity's struggle with addiction is a journey through the wilderness of idolatry where temptations, trials, and deprivations abound, but where God's grace is always available to guide, protect, empower, and transform us.... The power of grace flows most fully when human will chooses to act in harmony with divine will."[39]

7

TO THE ENDS OF THE EARTH

Seed Planting in the U.S.S.R.

A sower went out to sow. As he sowed, some seeds fell along the path, and the birds came and devoured them. Other seeds fell on rocky ground, where they had not much soil, and immediately they sprang up, since they had no depth of soil, but when the sun rose they were scorched; since they had no root they withered away. Other seeds fell upon thorns, and the thorns grew up and choked them. Other seeds fell on good soil and brought forth grain, some a hundredfold, some sixty, some thirty.

— Matthew 13:2–9 GNB

In 1983, one grateful recovering person from the West Coast was inspired like Bill W. to seed Alcoholics Anonymous in the Soviet Union. She convinced a group of other recovering individuals to work with her toward the goal of carrying the seeds of AA to the U.S.S.R. The name they gave themselves was "Create a Sober World," or CASW, as it has come to be called. The first group of anonymous individuals, including one family member of an alcoholic, made the first CASW trip in April 1986; membership in AA or Al-Anon was a prerequisite. They came from California, Connecticut, Hawaii, Idaho, Missouri, and Texas. At the same time other recovering alcoholics on the East Coast and elsewhere were also inspired to plant the seeds of the AA way of life in the Soviet Union. One is J. W. Canty, an Episcopal priest from New York. These risk takers made several trips to the Soviet Union and met with government officials and physicians, sometimes individually and sometimes in groups. The officials stated that they had no problem with their bringing AA into the Soviet Union, provided they had no personal agenda, engaged in no political discussions, and entered into no black market activity. They were greeted cordially and with interest by the Soviet physicians who invited them to visit their narcology hospitals.[1] After the trip a high school teacher from California decided to get training as a drug and alcohol counselor and return to live in the Soviet Union. He did so in 1989 and he has helped establish AA groups in Kiev, Kishniev, Odessa, Volgograd, Alma-Ata, and Moscow, and he has helped start Al-Anon and NA groups as well.

In April 1986, the first open AA speaker meetings were held in Kiev and Moscow. At one meeting in Moscow, the Soviets' response was, "We have a common problem; there is no common solution and we must work together."[2]

Time magazine indicates that J. W. Canty planted the seeds for the first AA in Moscow, known as the "Moscow Beginners" group, on a trip to the Soviet Union in 1985.[3] But there is some dissension about whether that is true, and this has led to rivalries among the recovering alcoholics in Moscow. The date given by Rev. Canty for the first Moscow AA meeting is August 16, 1987.[4] He credits himself with planting the seeds for AA in Siberia as well. Rev. Canty claims that he is doing "God's work," and so do the other anonymous individuals who have planted seeds through an organization called Volunteers of America.

Recovering alcoholics from Finland, too, have been actively planting seeds, encouraging and supporting the fledgling Soviet AA members. They travel to visit with the AA and Al-Anon groups in Leningrad and Moscow twice a year and invite members of these groups to visit their conventions, held four times a year, to stay in their homes, and to go to meetings in Helsinki.

One Finnish member of AA describes the treatment of alcoholism in the Soviet Union as punitive, or, in the words of Rev. Canty, alcoholics are treated as "non-persons."[5] Alcoholics have traditionally been hospitalized for six months. The standard method of treatment has been a combination of microwave resonance therapy, a type of electro-acupuncture and hypnosis called encoding, and cleansing of the blood through dialysis, which takes away the craving for alcohol or other drugs.[6] Then the alcoholic or drug abuser signs an abstinence pledge. Labeled as alcoholics for two years and given menial jobs at half pay under strict supervision, alcoholics rarely keep their sobriety for long. When they relapse they are sent back to the hospital. If the alcohol causes them to become violent or to break the law, they are sent to forced labor camps. There have been as many as 314 camps in the U.S.S.R. Efforts are being made currently to close down these labor camps. With the current state of political and economic unrest in the U.S.S.R., the number of alcohol-related crimes has risen. According to ABC reporter John Lawrence, there are an estimated two hundred thousand Soviets being held in hospitals and labor camps against their will.[7] According to Timo Leshinen, a Cobatshov Examination or survey revealed that in fifty factories in Moscow 50 percent of those who came to work Monday morning were totally drunk, and the "motive for coming to work was to get more vodka from the automatic vodka dispensing machine in the factories.[8] According to a narcologist in Kishniev, Moldavia 60 percent of the construction workers have problems with alcohol.[9]

One American visitor described a second visit to the Moscow Beginners' Group in 1988 as the highlight of her life. "The compassion and energy of hopeful recovery buoys me today. Perhaps the early meetings in Akron and New York felt like this."[10]

The message of recovery has been carried to family members on several trips. On each trip literature is taken from AA and Al-Anon headquarters in New York City. If that literature is in English, it is translated by a group member and hand-carried to another group. Meetings are held in homes and in rented meeting halls. American visitors share their experiences with their Soviet hosts in Vilnius, Lithunia, Moscow, Leningrad, Kiev, Kishniev, and other cities over cakes, candies, and tea served from a samovar. They find that the stories of the disease of alcoholism are the same, only the language is different.

In September 1988, the first meeting of AA in Leningrad took place. A recovering alcoholic from America, who was also a student in Russian literature, spent the fall of 1988 at Leningrad State University. She was worried about not having the fellowship of the program while she was there. But she managed to continue her twelve-step work by seeding several AA groups. Early in her stay in the U.S.S.R., she was invited by Petrahyevech, a Ph.D. scientist, and his wife, Tahmahrah, to meet with them in their flat to discuss alcoholism.[11] Petrahyevech had been able to stay sober by being part of a therapy group, but his wife didn't like him associating with the lowest members of society, i.e., alcoholics. But they both saw the fellowship and love offered by the program through their American guest. Now there is not only an AA meeting in Leningrad, but also an Al-Anon group started by Tahmahrah. Later, the American student started a meeting at a recovery ward in a narcological hospital.

One anonymous individual had been hospitalized seven times for his alcoholism, but his treatment had consisted only of interviews with psychologists and hard labor. "The doctors did not study in the same school as me," he told her after hearing the twelve steps. As he closed his eyes she saw a tiny spark of hope, the first hope he had in seventeen years.[12]

A research engineer was another recovering alcoholic inspired by the American volunteers to start an AA group, called the "Neva" group. He voluntarily sought help for his alcoholism and subjected himself to the usual Soviet form of treatment, but it didn't help, and he spent half of his life in and out of the forced labor camps. "The narcologists," he said, "consider us weak persons."[13] He found it easy to get narcotics at the labor camps. He even got his supply from the administrators. He joined an All-Union Optimologist Club, whose founder tried to put down AA and the twelve steps. He and his wife began inviting other alcoholics to take part in AA meetings in their two-room flat. While their baby, their eight-year-old daughter, and the grandmother tried to sleep, these fledgling twelve-steppers found that the steps helped them find unity. He has found that, even though he was an alcoholic, God still loves him! In the downward spiral of his disease he had often forgotten about God. In April 1989 his wife started Al-Anon and Al-Ateen meetings, which now meet in their local narcology hospital.

Anonymous individuals have been planting the seeds of the twelve-step AA way to recovery from alcoholism in the Soviet Union and other Eastern bloc countries since 1981, according to AA headquarters.[14] More than three hundred men and women in recovery have shared their stories in six of the Soviet Republics. AA and Al-Anon, NA and Al-Ateen are spreading rapidly. Monies are now being requested to translate the literature, but the best translators are the recovering members themselves. After hearing one member of the American group share his understanding of step 2, one member of an Al-Anon group translated the whole Al-Anon *One Day at a Time* booklet and presented him a copy when he returned the following year.

This author made two seed-planting trips to the Soviet Union, in October 1989 and again in March 1991. Not only recovery literature, but calligraphic copies of the Serenity Prayer as well as Russian-language editions of the New English Bible and the Serenity Bible went into my suitcase. Everywhere I looked for an opportunity to make contacts with persons who were either recovering from alcoholism or involved in treatment.

While our tour group was in Tbilisi, Georgia, in 1989, we learned that a two-year U.S.-Soviet work plan had been developed to work on alcohol and drug problems. In 1985, President Gorbachev had addressed the Soviet people, making a plea for the United States and the Soviet Union to work together to solve their common problem, alcoholism. First, radical measures were undertaken to limit the sales of alcoholic beverages. But the efforts were a disaster. The sale of sugar increased as people made their own moonshine and then there was a shortage of sugar. Many exchange visits were underway between U.S. delegations and Soviet delegations. Even though many new AA groups are being seeded by the U.S. delegations, communications are poor and the group meetings are not well publicized.

While our tour group was in Tbilisi, an opportunity arose for me to visit the home of the deputy in charge of health for the Tbilisi area. Over cakes and specially prepared dishes created by his wife, Nelly, I asked if it were possible to arrange to see an alcoholism treatment center. The next day our host arranged for several members of our group to visit the local narcological center in a mental health complex. We were ushered into a drab concrete building where the director of the center greeted us. There around a table with an interpreter, Dr. Gela Lezhava, a psychiatrist, talked about alcoholism in the Soviet Union. The alcoholism problem, he informed us, is a characteristic of the twentieth century. "It is caused by a deficit of life," he stated emphatically. According to Dr. Lezhava, alcohol use is a social problem and a Christian one, because the Christian religion gives one permission to drink wine. When I asked about AA, he said that the movement hadn't come to Georgia yet.

I left some literature, although I noted that someone had been there before me. He claimed that alcoholism was not a problem in their republic yet. But we had noted the many rounds of toasts with homemade vodka and wine that went on late into the night and the young men and women returning from the opera carrying bags of champagne and vodka into hotel rooms to drink themselves into oblivion in the wee hours of the morning. I hoped that the twelve-step one-day-at-a-time books we left at the treatment center with a copy of the Serenity Prayer would help some of these suffering individuals find sobriety and serenity, as well as hope. Just before my return trip to the Soviet Union, Nelly and her husband, Tamaz, came for a visit to Pittsburgh. I was able to return their hospitality by arranging for them to visit a Maternal Addictions Research Project and Adolescent Treatment Program at St. Francis Hospital. There they discovered that 20 percent of pregnant women are addicted to crack-cocaine and alcohol. They still did not understand that alcohol was a drug and they had not heard of crack-cocaine.

In Moscow, we met twice with a forty-year-old American who worked for the weekly *Moscow News*. Bob M. has spent seven years in Moscow, two as a graduate student of Russian language and literature and six as a copyeditor for the *Moscow News*. He asked first for one of the Bibles I had brought with me. "I gave my last Bible away," he said. "It was my personal copy, and I have been praying about where I could get another one."[15] I gave him three of the Russian Bibles I had brought in my suitcase. He shared his story with me as he led us through the maze of the Moscow subway system and around the rain-filled potholes in the deteriorating sidewalks and streets of Moscow.

Bob had left the U.S. Navy and his job on a nuclear submarine base drydock in Scotland. As a conscientious objector and Christian pacifist, he had first come to the Soviet Union in 1980. Here is a young man, I thought to myself, who is trying to live his idealism. He saw his job at the *Moscow News* as trying to make the newspaper articles, printed in English, more honest and more effective. He also has started three chapters of Toastmaster's International in Moscow. Once having a phobia of public speaking, Bob is becoming a regular public speaker, teaching the Soviets his newly learned skills as well. His main purpose is to promote freedom of speech in the U.S.S.R. and to be a bridge between American and Soviet Toastmasters.

Bob talked to me about the hardships of life in the Soviet Union, the standing in line for food and clothes, and the poor quality of goods. He made about $2,000 a year. When I met him again in 1991, he poignantly expressed how difficult it was going to be to live on his fixed income salary while the cost of living was escalating. He spoke with sadness of his father's death. His father was a recovering alcoholic and a lifelong member of AA, he claimed. When I inquired about how to find an AA meeting on my first trip, he was unable to locate the meeting places of the Moscow groups. After our first meeting in 1989, I gave him a copy of the Serenity Prayer, which he had seen often on his father's wall, as well as *One Day at a Time,* a book for recovering ACOAs, and urged him to join a church group. Bob, like many Adult Children of Alcoholics, has intense missionary zeal. During my second trip, in 1991, I gave him the name of the local Al-Anon contact and urged him to seek there the companionship he needed to renew his courage and strength in order to survive.

After my first trip in 1989, I decided I needed to share and return the hospitality of my Soviet hosts in the U.S.S.R. A joint conference of the Chautauqua Institute and the University of Pittsburgh was taking place in Pittsburgh the next week and alcoholism and other drug research and treatment were to be discussed at the conference.[16] I made many phone calls to both the conference planners and the treatment community in Pittsburgh and arrangements were made not only to host the Soviet visitors for a luncheon but to visit the St. Francis Hospital Maternal Addictions Research Project and Dr. Shirley Hill's Genetic Alcoholism Research Project. There Dr. Valentina Maskalenko met a fellow researcher. She had only read about Dr. Hill's research but now she was able to talk face-to-face with a colleague.

At the public forums during the conference, Dr. Janis Strazdinsh of Latvia thanked AA for sending delegations to Latvia and helping to start four AA groups. Spirituality is extremely important to recovery, he noted.[17] Dr. Valiant of Dartmouth College stated that the cheapest and most effective kind of treatment for alcoholism still costs only a dollar a meeting in the U.S.A. and only a few rubles in the Soviet Union.

Dr. Valentina Moskalenko and I talked in the car between events, sharing our interest in family members affected by the disease of alcoholism. As chief of the genetics division of the All-Union Scientific Center of Medico-Biological Problems of Addiction in Moscow, she was interested in any literature I could provide for her to learn about the effect of the disease of alcoholism on family members. She had started an Al-Anon group at her hospital and was particularly interested in co-dependency as a pathology. In our short time together, we exchanged ideas on our common interest in treating family members, and she returned to Moscow with several current books and papers on co-dependency. I then sent on her name to Bob M. with the information that there was now support for family members of recovering alcoholics. On my return trip in 1991, Dr. Moskalenko and I met for dinner and again shared our common interest in co-dependency. She was now working on a research project with young children of alcoholics, as was I. We then attended a regional Al-Anon meeting together. Having written an article entitled "Should I Marry an Alcoholic?" in a popular Soviet family magazine, she now receives tons of fan mail and has become the Soviet equivalent of Claudia Black!

Mr. Rick Esterly, CEO of the Caron Foundation, believes that the twelve-step movement will take off in the Soviet Union because the people are deeply spiritual.[18] The Chit Chat Treatment Center has helped to set up a thirty-bed treatment unit in Narcological Hospital No. 17 in Moscow. That hospital has a network of treatment centers stretching across Moscow. Salus International Health Institute is now coordinating and funding that effort.[19] The director of that program attempts to approach alcoholism and addiction from a body-mind-spirit perspective.[20] There is also interest in starting an adolescent program and prevention programs in the schools. Opportunities abound now for treatment and training in the Soviet Union.

As of spring 1991, there are thirty-three registered AA groups in some fourteen cities in the Soviet Union. They held their first intergroup conference in Minsk, Byelorussia, in November 1990. Eleven registered Al-Anon meetings are in existence; six of those are meeting regularly in Moscow.

For the Soviets, the twelve-step programs provide a way to end the oppressive fashion alcoholism has been treated in their country. They are discovering through the twelve-step groups how democracy works. They are discovering that they are human beings of value and that they can find freedom in surrendering to a Higher Power, whom many choose to call God. Many raised as atheists are finding that their Higher Power is Love as it is expressed through the caring and sharing of the groups. For others, who secretly attended church services under communist repression, the twelve-step way of life is uniquely compatible with their spiritual beliefs.[21]

The rewards for those who have planted the seeds for recovery are gifts of love. One anonymous individual said that his reward came in knowing that the AA program works everywhere. "It is always amazing to see hope come alive." My reward came in hearing stories of those who had been suffering from someone else's alcohol and drug abuse and have permission for the first time to regain balance in their lives and to take care of themselves. Smiles and hugs helped them to find hope and a new freedom in recovery.

Through the sharing and caring of many anonymous individuals we were able to pass on to others some new beginnings. We were able to do what governments bogged down in bureaucracy are unable to do.

Our seed planting is now bringing forth seedlings, which will become mature new trees, that will provide life and hope for the world.

Crossbreeds: Other "A" Groups

> I doubt if the Twelve Steps that have changed the course of existence for so many thousands of lives could have been the product of human insight and observation. And they can and will bless anyone, alcoholic or not, who will follow them through and be obedient to them. They are morally and spiritually and psychologically and practically as sound as can be.
>
> — Sam Shoemaker

In the 1990s these prophetic words ring true! People flock back to churches and synagogues, about fifteen million of them, not to attend services, but support groups instead. In the last ten years the number of self-help organizations has quadrupled; groups existed for almost every conceivable problem.[22] We have become a pathological nation trying to recover. Divorce, drugs, the failed yuppie quest for perfection, and dysfunctional families have left people feeling alone and miserable. To be recovering from something makes us feel that we belong. Still looked on with skepticism by the professional psychotherapists and physicians, the self-help movement has been shown to prolong life.[23] But some of the professionals who have criticized the self-help movement have some legitimate concerns. Marian Walters states her reservations about the co-dependency movement:

> I am concerned about the co-dependency movement's promulgation of the disease model to explain a vast array of human behaviors; the use of what is essentially a medical term — addiction — to describe activities as disparate as substance abuse, loving, gambling, shopping, sex, incest, lateness, intimacy, affairs, relationships, eating, worrying, work, and more.[24]

She goes on to say that the disease model, which calls the excesses of many ordinary human behaviors "addictive," clouds our understanding of the really addictive behaviors associated with chemical dependency. It means, she adds, that we must have a prescription, a formula to follow, for our very humanness! Wendy Kaminer criticizes the co-dependency movement because it masks evil as sickness while enabling publishers to make lots of money. She links it to the narcissism of the 1970s but says:

"This isn't the narcissism commonly associated with self-help so much as submission; it isn't individualism as much as a hunger to belong."[25]

Those who counsel individuals and family members of alcoholics and drug addicts have found the definition of co-dependency helpful in describing those who try to control and fix the addict, taking the responsibility away from him or her. To find a way to help family members to begin to focus on themselves instead of the addict was the original intent of the co-dependency movement. But now the notion of co-dependency has been taken to an extreme as it is being used to classify 95 percent of the American public. An important area of research is to refine and define the pathology. One should be careful to use the term in an appropriate context.

In this chapter I discuss selected twelve-step groups that can help survivors of substance abuse and the physical and sexual abuse often associated with it. In the next chapter, I will specifically address ways that some churches are beginning to incorporate the twelve steps into the ongoing life of the church.

Al-Anon

It was Annie S., wife of Dr. Bob, who first began to comfort other wives with these words, "Come in, my dear, you're among friends now — friends who understand."[26] First the relatives of alcoholics accompanied them to meetings. It wasn't until 1950 that Bill W. suggested that his wife, Lois, open an office to provide service for the many family groups that were springing up all over the United States and Canada. Concern for the problems of children surfaced in 1955, and in 1957 the first Alateen group began. Al-Anon family groups, which include not only Alateen but Adult Children of Alcoholics as well, help family members relearn how to reflect on their lives using the same twelve steps and traditions as AA They experience how not to wallow in self-pity and how they too have become involved in the disease of alcoholism and need to recover.

> The Al-Anon Family Groups are a fellowship of relatives and friends of alcoholics who share their experience, strength and hope in order to solve their common problems. We believe that alcoholism is a family illness and that changed attitudes can aid recovery.

> The Al-Anon is not allied with any sect, denomination, political entity, organization or institution; does not engage in any controversy, neither endorses or opposes any cause. There are no dues for membership. Al-Anon is self-supporting through its own voluntary contributions.
>
> Al-Anon has but one purpose: to help families of alcoholics. We do this by practicing the twelve steps, by welcoming and giving comfort to families of alcoholics, and by giving understanding and encouragement to the alcoholic.[27]

Family members learn to detach, not to become emotionally involved with the results of the illness, not to make the addict act as they want them to, to keep an open mind and a closed mouth, to stop participating in the "games" that the addict plays, and to allow their loved ones to make their mistakes. They come to realize that "there but for the grace of God go I," that no situation is too difficult to be bettered, that there is hope in the midst of despair.

Gamblers Anonymous

Tim was a twenty-four-year old college graduate who first started gambling when his dad took him to the bar and he played the video games while his dad drank. By the time he went to his first twelve-step meeting, he had stolen money from his sister to support his gambling habit as well as his alcohol addiction. He hit his bottom when he ended up on the streets and had to sleep in a shelter for homeless men. He compared his first few meetings of Gamblers Anonymous with his first few meetings at Alcoholics Anonymous as going from the glamorous to the everyday. "All the men at the Gamblers Anonymous meetings have flashy clothes and jewelry," he reported.

Of the 80 percent of the American public who gamble, some are pathological gamblers. As gambling has become legal, the number of pathological gamblers has increased. The American Psychiatric Association defines pathological gambling as a "disorder of impulse control."[28] Pathological gamblers seek action; they are risk takers and thrill seekers. They are obsessed with getting even. The disease has three phases: the adventurous or winning phase, the losing phase, and the desperation phase.[29] The gambler's family suffers in the same way as an alcoholic's family does and needs treatment and support in the same way as well.

Trust and the feeling of being betrayed are two issues that need to be addressed by family members in the recovery process.

Narcotics Anonymous

> NA is a non-profit fellowship or society of men and women for whom drugs had become a major problem. We are recovering addicts who meet regularly to help each other to stay clean. This is a program of complete abstinence from all drugs. There is only one requirement for membership, the desire to stop using. We suggest that you keep an open mind and give yourself a break. Our program is a set of principles written so simply that we can follow them in our daily lives. The most important thing about them is that: THEY WORK.[30]

Narcotics Anonymous follows much the same format as Alcoholics Anonymous. Before NA was formed, drug addicts attending Alcoholics Anonymous meetings found that their addictive disease was similar to but different from that of alcoholics. In July 1953, the first meeting of NA was held in Southern California. The World Service Office was formed in 1972 and helped bring unity and a sense of purpose to the fledgling fellowship.[31] The first step in NA speaks of powerlessness over drugs and addicts talk about staying clean instead of staying sober. These addicts found that they could not use any mind-altering drug, including marijuana, alcohol, and prescription drugs. Those addicted to both drugs and alcohol should attend both types of meetings.

Each addictive drug has a different effect on the brain chemistry. Cocaine "fries" the brain, marijuana "confuses" the brain, "ice" or methamphetamine hydrochloride "deludes" the brain, and alcohol "sogs" the brain. Valium and Xanax, still commonly prescribed tranquilizers, can give a person seizures with overdoses or when their usage is withdrawn. Each of these drugs and many others, including antihistamines, are mind-altering and if abused lead to addiction. They all deplete the brain of needed neurotransmitters. Some cause extensive physical damage to other body organs. Drug addicts often have a difficult time in early recovery because of the intensity of the depression that is part of the withdrawal process and the healing of the brain.

Overeaters Anonymous

> Overeaters Anonymous is a Fellowship of individuals who, through shared experience and mutual support, are recovering from compulsive overeating.
>
> We welcome everyone who wants to stop eating compulsively. There are no dues or fees for members; we are self-supporting through our own contributions, neither soliciting nor accepting outside donations. OA is not affiliated with any public or private organization, political movement, ideology or religious doctrine; we take no position on outside issues.
>
> Our primary purpose is to abstain from compulsive overeating and to carry this message of recovery to those who still suffer.[32]

Overeaters Anonymous, formed in 1960, is a twelve-step recovery program patterned after Alcoholics Anonymous. The group has changed the terms "alcohol" and "alcoholic" to "food" and "compulsive overeater." Like alcoholism, compulsive overeating is an emotional, physical, and spiritual illness. Overeaters is not another fad diet club that makes its money from desperate individuals, both men and women, who try over and over again to lose or gain weight through the diet-and-calories approach. Some even go through a surgical process to reduce the size of their stomachs, called a "tummy tuck," before they try OA.

Like alcoholics who drink out of control, overeaters have a compulsion to eat out of control. Their eat to fill voids and deal with negative emotions. Their physiological disease comes from a metabolic deficiency called sugar dysmetabolism. Bulimics binge and often purge. Anorexics exhibit controlled noneating patterns and compulsive exercising. The consumption of carbohydrates and refined sugar gives them a false sense of well-being, followed by depression. Abstinence, then, simply means staying away from compulsive overeating and that means for some avoiding refined sugar and carbohydrates.[33] Although OA members do not practice any particular diet, OA advises its members who are interested in specific nutritional food plans to consult qualified professionals. Overeaters have extreme problems of control, even though most of the time their eating is out of control. They delude themselves into thinking that they are self-sufficient despite their dependent behavior and often suicidal thoughts.

Overeaters encourage the use of a sponsor who can be called at any hour of the day or night if the urge to eat compulsively returns. Overeaters' only relationship is with food. They live to eat instead of eating to live. Undereaters have the same problem only in reverse. They control by not eating and live to not eat instead of eating to live. They are two extremes of the same illness. The illness often develops in alcoholic or emotionally dysfunctional families.

Both overeaters and undereaters can benefit and learn about recovery by attending Overeaters Anonymous meetings. The emphasis is not on weight loss but on abstinence one day at a time and finding a new and healthy relationship with food.

Sex and Love Addicts Anonymous

> The only requirement for membership is a desire to stop living out a pattern of sex and love addiction. SLAA is supported entirely through contributions of its membership, and is free to all who need it.
>
> To counter the destructive consequences of sex and love addiction we draw on four major resources:
>
> 1. Our willingness to stop acting out in our own personal bottom line addictive behavior on a daily basis.
> 2. Our capacity to reach out for the supportive fellowship within SLAA.
> 3. Our practice of the Twelve Step program of recovery to achieve sexual and emotional sobriety.
> 4. Our developing a relationship with a Power greater than ourselves which can guide and sustain in recovery.[34]

Meetings of sex and love addicts provide safe places to be honest about sexually compulsive actions and problems of emotional dependency. Each individual's recovery, of course, is a very intimate personal matter, but extended periods of sobriety or abstinence are advocated. The keys to recovery are learning to love oneself, finding a sponsor who understands, and following the same twelve-step format of recovery as Alcoholics Anonymous. Another such group is Sexaholics Anonymous. It encourages sex addicts to stay committed in heterosexual relationships.

These are just a few of the twelve-step support groups available for those who acknowledge one of these problems. There are some differences in wording but not in substance. There is one thing these groups have in common: they all acknowledge that by themselves they cannot help themselves but with others they can get better!

> Almighty God, you have given us grace at this time with one accord to make our common supplication to you; and you have promised through your well-beloved son that when two or three are gathered together in his Name you will be in the midst of them:
>
> Fulfill now, O Lord, our desires and petitions as may be best for us; granting us in this world knowledge of your truth, and in the age to come life everlasting.
>
> — St. John Chrysostom

TWELVE-STEP GROUPS
A Selected List

Al-Anon Family Groups
P.O. Box 862, Midtown Station
New York, NY 10118
(212) 302-7240

Alcoholics Anonymous World Services, Inc.
Box 459, Grand Central Station
New York, NY 10017
(212) 686-1100

Co-Dependents Anonymous
P.O. Box 33577
Phoenix, AZ 85067-3577
(602) 944-0141

Gamblers Anonymous
National Service Office
P.O. Box 17173
Los Angeles, CA 90017
(213) 386-8789

Narcotics Anonymous
World Service Office
P.O. Box 9999
Van Nuys, CA 91409
(818) 780-3951

Overeaters Anonymous
4025 Spencer, #203
Torrance, CA 90503
(213) 542-8363

Sex and Love Addicts Anonymous
P.O. Box 1964
Boston, MA 02105
(617) 625-7961

Nicotine Anonymous
2118 Greenwich Street
San Francisco, CA 94123
(415) 922-8575

8

THE CHURCH AND THE "A" GROUPS: MUTUAL CHALLENGE

Hunger for Community

An article appeared in the *United Methodist Reporter*, December 30, 1988, written by Clay Oglesbee. The question he posed was this: "Will twelve-step groups like Alcoholics Anonymous replace Christianity?" Three years later, the rapid growth of twelve-step groups all over the world leads us to wonder if the answer to that question might be yes. So-called twelve-step churches are beginning to appear. One in St. Paul, Minnesota, calls itself the "new Christianity." Another group in Addison, Pennsylvania, calls itself the "Lord's Earth Church" from the Lord's Prayer, "Thy Kingdom come, thy will be done, on earth as it is in heaven."

Any student of church history will tell us that many splinter groups have broken off from the main body of the church. Some of these have ended up as heresies, others have become separate denominations. By the grace of God, Christianity has managed to survive and thrive, sometimes in new forms, sometimes in revived old forms. If the group is heretical it eventually dies. In medieval days, those who challenged the church to change were burned at the stake. Martin Luther started out by challenging the Roman Catholic Church to reform and the Lutheran Church evolved as a result. The Anabaptists broke away at the time of the Reformation; the Amish and Mennonites resulted. John Wesley broke away from the tradition of the Church of England, formed small group Methodist societies, and ordained lay preachers. The Methodist Church resulted. At first the Anglican Church was established in North America and was the predominant denomination throughout the thirteen colonies. But soon thereafter the United States was pluralistic in its various forms of worshipping God.

Throughout the history of the United States religious leaders have arisen who have taken up social causes and founded new sects. Prohibition and the temperance movement resulted from the evangelistic efforts of some of these church leaders: Lyman Beecher (1775–1863), Francis Willard (1839–98), and Billy Sunday (1862–1935). The Washingtonians evolved from this prohibition-temperance movement. These religious leaders and others who wanted to prohibit the sale of alcoholic beverages helped these groups of drunks stay sober. But their control also helped speed their demise and no new sect was formed.

Traced in this book is the development of similar groups of drunks trying to stay sober. They were helped by evangelical Protestant and Catholic religious leaders who did not want to prohibit the sale of alcoholic beverages. Their interest was to help these drunks stay sober through Christian community. Considering their origins, it is not remarkable that these twelve-step support groups and others like them are still flourishing fifty years later. Dr. John Rodgers, former Dean of Trinity School for Ministry, put it this way: "The Twelve Steps are surely one of the most powerful ways the Holy Spirit is presently touching people, alienated from the Church and shaped by our secular culture, to bring them into vital contact with the Lord."[1]

We are no longer a nation that prides itself in our freedom to worship God but instead in our freedom from the worship of God. Even those who follow twelve-step programs are careful to explain that they are in a spiritual recovery program and not a religious one. "There is no rivalry between religion and recovery," according to Clay Oglesbee. "Both are 'earthen vessels' bearing a too neglected treasure: wholeness and new intimacy with ourselves, with others, and with God."[2] Yet those who attend twelve-step meetings are disillusioned with organized religion in its present denominational structure. The future will tell us whether any new sects will arise out of the twelve-step movement.

People in the late twentieth century are hungry for this intimacy found in the community of fellow sufferers. They so desperately want to be accepted, to belong to a community. Philip Turner, in a paper entitled "Spirituality in the Parish: An Anglican Perspective," states that churches are less and less communities of memory and hope and more and more collections of individuals who belong for reasons of their own." Robert Bellah, in *Habits of the Heart*, says that when this happens, religious belief becomes a private and eclectic affair.[3] In other words, churches are buildings where we come to be blessed by the minister and expect to pay our dues, like belonging to a club. But life is not like that; and so alcoholics have found, the hard way, that life can be better by sharing their pain with one another, by holding each other accountable, and by accepting failure and starting again. It is not a new brand of Christianity but a recapturing of the old original brand.

Twelve-steppers who are discouraged with the church and are finding that ACOA and other twelve-step groups meet an unfulfilled longing to be accepted and to belong would do well to study the early heresies of the church and to examine their own character defects, such as rebelliousness, stubbornness, and problems with authority figures. They would do well to reflect on the passage from Paul's epistle to the Romans that says, "since they did not know the righteousness that comes from God and sought to establish their own, they did not submit to God's righteousness" (Rom. 10:3). The church is still the Body of Christ, no matter how flawed it is. It has survived for two thousand years, with its core of orthodoxy, bringing the Good News of Jesus Christ's birth, death, and resurrection and offering *metanoia*. The twelve steps came from the Christian message of atonement and redemption. Twelve-step group service boards, in order to encourage the worship of God on the Sabbath, might consider discouraging twelve-step meetings during worship times. These "born again" Higher Power folks might just be the salt and leaven to revitalize these places of worship.

At a time when institutional religion is struggling to survive, it might be open to being educated about the twelve-step programs, about addiction and recovery and desire to attract those who feel disenfranchised by institutional religion back into the mainstream of religious life. The following are a few examples of how this is currently being done.

ACO Almighty

A ministry of the Episcopal Church of the Savior in Ambridge, Pennsylvania, is called the Lazarus Center. This group meets Tuesday evenings and attracts those who grew up in dysfunctional homes. Its aim is to review the promises of God and to help persons get in touch with common feelings, thoughts, and behavior patterns associated with growing up in these homes.

ACO ALMIGHTY, The Lazarus Center, 1200 Merchant St., Ambridge, PA 15003; (412) 266-4412.

Overcomers

A Christian support group for the chemically dependent and their families, Overcomers is a ministry of the Whittier Baptist Church in Southern California. They believe that their Higher Power is Jesus Christ. Their fivefold purpose is:

1. To provide fellowship in recovery.
2. To be and to live reconciled to God and his family.
3. To gain a better understanding of alcohol and mood-altering chemicals and the disease of addiction.
4. To be built up and strengthened in our faith in Christ.
5. To render dedicated service to others who are suffering as we once suffered.[4]

They practice the twelve steps of AA and Al-Anon and combine Bible study with the twelve steps. They believe that alcoholics can be F.R.E.E.D.[5] of the disease of alcoholism and that God will supply the tools.

OVERCOMERS OUTREACH, 17027 E. Janison Dr., Whittier, CA 90603; (213) 697-2368

Recovery Works

Recovery Works is a new ministry of St. John the Divine in Houston, Texas, which integrates Christian spirituality and the twelve steps. It focuses on education support, renewal, and referrals for clergy and lay alike. Its programs include Sunday school classes, retreats, dinner fellowships, lectures and conferences, curriculum development, spiritual direction, and counseling.

RECOVERY WORKS, St. John the Divine, 2450 River Oaks Blvd., Houston, TX 77019; (713) 622-3600

Lion Tamers Anonymous

This group meets every Sunday evening at the First United Methodist Church in Peoria, Illinois. It is a Christian twelve-step program and bases its program on (1) encouragement, (2) fellowship, and (3) healing.

It has seven goals: (1) anonymity, (2) confidence, (3) charitableness, (4) continuance, (5) commitment, (6) referral, and (7) education. It reaches out to recovering alcoholics, co-dependents, adult children of alcoholics, and adult children from dysfunctional families.

LION TAMERS ANONYMOUS, First United Methodist Church, 116 N.E. Perry Ave., Peoria, IL 61603; (309) 673-3641 or (309) 274-5595

This is just a sampling of those churches that have begun to incorporate the twelve steps into their outreach ministry. The Church of the Resurrection in Mars, Pennsylvania, has a preaching, teaching, and counseling ministry centered around a Christianized version of the twelve steps, and the church is growing. The rector, the Rev. Bill Eaton, has brought the "A" groups out of the basement and into the sanctuary.

Sam Shoemaker has this to say to the church about what it needs to learn from AA: "Nobody gets anywhere till he recognizes a clearly defined need, men are redeemed in a life-changing fellowship, there is a necessity for definite personal dealing with people, for facing ourselves as we really are, and for a real change of heart or conversion." He calls AA a society of the "before and after,"[6] a group of ordinary men and women with great need who have found a great Answer and do not hesitate to make it known wherever they can.[7] Alison Barfoot says that "when we give ourselves to staying in fellowship and working at our relationships even when there are differences, we pay homage to the King of kings."[8]

Twelve Steps for Christian Living

Imagine there are Christians and God-seekers all over the world gathered together in small groups around a program like the following twelve steps for Christian living prepared by the Institute for Christian living. They have all come from twelve-step groups, which were formed to solve specific problems, only these fellowships have led them to wanting to be in closer communion with God. It will be the inbreaking of the kingdom of heaven and the Ultimate Answer to our cry for help:

> In my distress I called out to the Lord,
> I cried to my God for help.
> From his temple he heard my voice;
> my cry came before him, into his ears.
> (Ps. 18:6 NIV)

THE TWELVE STEPS OF CHRISTIAN LIVING

1. We admit that we need God's gift of salvation, that we are powerless over certain areas of our lives and that our lives are at times sinful and unmanageable.
2. We came to believe through the Holy Spirit that a power that came from the person of Jesus Christ and that is greater than ourselves can transform our weaknesses into strengths.
3. We made a decision to turn our will and our lives over to the care of Christ as we understand Him — hoping to understand Him more fully.
4. We made a searching and fearless moral inventory of ourselves — both our strengths and our weaknesses.
5. We admit to Christ, to ourselves and to another human being the exact nature of our sins.
6. We became entirely ready to have Christ heal all these defects of character that prevent us from having a more spiritual lifestyle.
7. We humbly ask Christ to transform all our shortcomings.
8. We made a list of all people we have harmed and become willing to make amends to them all.
9. We make direct amends to such people wherever possible, except when to do so would injure them or others.
10. We continue to take personal inventory and, when we are wrong, promptly admit it and, when we are right, thank God for His guidance.
11. We seek through prayer and meditation to improve our conscious contact with Christ as we understand Him, praying for knowledge of His will for us and the power to carry that out.
12. Having experienced a new sense of spirituality as a result of these steps and realizing that this sense is a gift of God's grace, we are willing to share the message of His love and forgiveness with others and to practice these principles for spiritual living in all our affairs.[9]

NOTES

The New Beginning: Introduction

1. Presiding Bishop of the Episcopal Church Edmond Browning coined the phrase in a talk at the Anglican Fellowship of Prayer Conference in Pittsburgh, June 1989.

2. Ernest Kurtz, *Not-God: A History of Alcoholics Anonymous* (Center City, Minn.: Hazelden, 1979); Nan Robertson, *Getting Better: Inside Alcoholics Anonymous* (New York: William Morrow, 1988).

3. *Alcoholics Anonymous Comes of Age* (New York: Alcoholics Anonymous World Services, Inc., 1957), 270.

4. Ibid., 254–61.

5. In 1976, the American Medical Association identified alcoholism as a disease with characteristic symptoms. In 1987 the *Diagnostic and Statistical Manual of Mental Disorders* (*DSM III R*), the American Psychiatric Association's guidelines for diagnosis of mental illness, classified psychoactive substance abuse and dependence with appropriate symptomatology (167–69). But they left out the spiritual component of this symptomatology, which I have described as follows: loss of spirituality and violation of one's moral principles, which may include discontinuing attendance at worship services. Their definition also does not include the following: (a) rationalization and projection as defenses; anger when usage is discussed; (b) mood swings and personality changes; the Jekyll and Hyde syndrome; (c) social and marital problems: sexual inadequacies, financial difficulties, deteriorating job performance. Eating disorders are also classified in *DSM III R* (65–69). These disorders are being effectively treated through the twelve-step approach just as psychoactive substance disorders are. Even compulsive sexual activity can be treated and arrested the twelve-step way.

6. Gerald May, *Addiction and Grace* (New York: Harper & Row, 1988), 3–4

1 / Roots

1. *Came to Believe*, 3.

2. *Alcoholics Anonymous Comes of Age*, 63.

3. This kind of spiritual experience is called a *theophany*. Moses had such an experience of God's voice in the burning bush, and on the top of Mt. Horeb he wrote the Ten Commandments. Isaiah saw God's glory and had a glimpse of

heaven. Jacob saw the angels ascending and descending on a ladder to heaven. Some addiction specialists might explain this experience as only hallucination.

4. *Alcoholics Anonymous Comes of Age*, 60. Helen Smith Shoemaker, *I Stand by the Door: The Life of Sam Shoemaker* (New York: Harper & Row, 1967), 192.

5. Ernest Kurtz, *Not-God*, 95; *Alcoholics Anonymous Comes of Age*, 46.

6. *As Bill Sees It* (New York: Alcoholics Anonymous World Services, Inc., 1967), 9.

7. Kurtz, *Not-God*, 49; Nan Robertson, *Getting Better: Inside Alcoholics Anonymous*, 58.

8. Robertson, *Getting Better*, 60.

9. *Alcoholics Anonymous Comes of Age*, 74.

10. Robertson, *Getting Better*, 58–59; Kurtz, *Not-God*, 45–47.

11. Kurtz, *Not-God*, 47.

12. *Alcoholics Anonymous Comes of Age*, 261.

13. Samuel Shoemaker, *Those Twelve Steps*, New York, Alcoholics Anonymous World Services, Inc., reprinted from *The Grapevine*, January 1964, 2.

14. Helen Smith Shoemaker, *I Stand by the Door*, 188.

15. Kurtz, *Not-God*, 98. The Spiritual Exercises of St. Ignatius, the founder of the Society of Jesus in 1548, were later to become the spiritual rule of the Jesuits.

16. *Alcoholics Anonymous Comes of Age*, 38.

17. Al-Anon Family Group Headquarters, Inc., New York, 1972.

18. The traditional form of the Lord's Prayer found in the Episcopal Prayer Book.

19. *Amida* is the Jewish prayer form of eighteen benedictions required to be said three times a day, each followed by "Amen." They were memorized by topic.

20. Evelyn Underhill, *ABBA, Meditations Based on the Lord's Prayer* (London: Longman Group Limited, 1940), 12.

21. Moshe Chaim Luzzatto, "An Essay in Fundamentals," *The Way of God* (Jerusalem and New York: Feldheim Publishers, 1983), 377.

22. Hymn 707, *The Hymnal 1982* (New York: Church Pension Fund, 1985).

23. The Greek word is *epiusios*, which means sufficient for the nearest future, not too much, but enough to relieve any concerns about the future.

24. *Rosh Ha-Shanah* is the Jewish New Year begins at sunset on September 24. It is called the Day of the Sounding of the Shofar, or Ram's Horn, or the Day of Remembering in the Scriptures (Lev. 23:24 and Num. 29:1). The Ram's Horn, when sounded one hundred times, aroused souls to repentance. The Day of Remembering reminds devout Jews of God's kingship and all His deeds for Israel. The period between Rosh Ha-Shanah and Yom Kipper is called the Ten Days of Repentance. It is a time for Jews to review their actions of the past year and to renew themselves by struggling with the negative aspects of their personalities.

25. A variation of a prayer of repentance found in Rabbi Nosson Scherman, *The Complete Art Scroll Siddur* (New York: Mesorah Publications, 1985), 825.

26. Eric P. Wheeler, "The Way of Perfection," *Dorotheos of Gasa* (Kalamazoo, Mich.: Cistercian Publications, 1977), chap. 26.

27. Underhill, *ABBA, Meditations Based on the Lord's Prayer*, 84.

28. Robert McAfee Brown, *The Legacy of Reinhold Niebuhr* (Chicago: University of Chicago Press, 1975), 3, 38.

29. Born in 1892, Reinhold Niebuhr was ordained a Lutheran minister and served as pastor of the Bethel Evangelical Church in Detroit, a largely German-American white-collar congregation. In the 1920s, the congregation, under Dr. Niebuhr's leadership, took an interest in social and political questions. A particular concern of Dr. Niebuhr's, along with his friend and mentor Episcopal Bishop of Michigan Charles Williams, was his challenge to Henry Ford and other industrialists to protect the rights of the unions to organize. In 1928, Dr. Niebuhr became professor of applied Christian ethics at Union Theological Seminary. His summer residence was in Heath, Massachusetts, where many theologians and clergy spent their summers.

30. Chautauqua at Pitt conference, Pittsburgh, Pa., November 3, 1989.

31. Malta, December 3, 1989. President Bush quoted from a version that said: "Don't worry about the things you can't do anything about."

32. AA summary of the Serenity Prayer origin, 1976; McCauley, *The Book of Prayers* (New York: Crown Publishers, 1954); George Appleton, ed. *The Oxford Book of Prayers* (New York: Oxford University Press, 1985); John Wallace Suter, *Prayers for a New World* (New York: Charles Scribner's Sons, 1964); and a collection of prayers by Niebuhr's wife, Ursula.

33. Leo Booth, *Spirituality and Recovery* (Deerfield Beach, Fla.: Health Communications, 1985).

34. Misty J. Thigpen, "The Not-So-Serene Origins of the Serenity Prayer," *Professional Counselor* (November–December 1989): 51–52, 83.

35. In a conversation with Seith Kastern, research librarian at Union Theological Seminary in November 1989. Dr. Niebuhr took credit for the original authorship of the Serenity Prayer (the first part of the prayer) in a letter to Sister M. Bernard Joseph of Mount St. Mary College, 1964, and in a letter to Mr. Hilborn in December 1965 (in the first letter the date of the prayer's origin was 1934; in the second, 1938). His wife, Ursula, claimed he wrote the prayer in the 1940s. Dr. Niebuhr copyrighted the prayer and received royalties from Hallmark Cards when they printed the prayer commercially in 1962. Dr. Niebuhr began to question his own authorship a few years later in 1970.

36. David L. Berquam, "Old Business," *The Exchange*, Reference and Adult Services Division, vol. 18, no. 2 (Winter 1978): 183–84.

37. *Alcoholics Anonymous Comes of Age*, 196.

38. Some Germans, many of whom have the German translation of the Serenity Prayer hanging above their fireplaces, claim that it was authored by Johann Christoph Oetinger, dean in Weinsberg from 1762 to 1769. Still others say that the German version was the work of Theodor Wilhelm, who used the pseudonym Oetinger and translated the Serenity Prayer into German after receiving a copy from a Canadian friend in the 1940s.

39. *Alcoholics Anonymous Comes of Age*, 196.
40. AA summary of the Serenity Prayer origin, 1976.
41. Ibid.
42. Brown, *Legacy*, 4. On Niebuhr see also Richard Wightman Fox, *Reinhold Niebuhr: A Biography* (New York: Pantheon, 1985), and Ronald H. Stone, *Reinhold Niebuhr: Prophet to Politicians* (Nashville: Abingdon Press, 1972).
43. *As Bill Sees It*, 20.
44. Another of Reinhold Niebuhr's prayers that has particular significance to the attitude of surrender so important in recovery is: "Oh Lord, who has taught us that to gain the whole world and to lose our souls is great folly, grant us the grace so to lose ourselves that we may truly find ourselves anew in the life of grace, and so to forget ourselves that we may be remembered in your kingdom" (*The Oxford Book of Prayers*, ed. George Appleton [New York: Oxford University Press, 1985], 119).

2 / The Trunk

1. Leonard U. Blumberg with William L. Pittman, *Beware of the First Drink* (Seattle, Wash.: Glen Abbey Books, 1991), 183.
2. Robertson, *Getting Better*, 57–58.
3. Shoemaker, *I Stand by the Door*, 176.
4. Irving Harris, *The Breeze of the Spirit: Sam Shoemaker and the Story of Faith at Work* (New York: Seabury Press, 1978), 87.
5. Shoemaker, *I Stand by the Door*, 177.
6. Garth Lean, *On the Tail of a Comet: The Life of Frank Buchman* (Colorado Springs, Colo.: Helmers and Howard Publishers, 1988), 155–62.
7. The enthusiasm of the Oxford Groupers did not convince the church hierarchy. In January 1935, two bishops in the Anglican Church, Dr. Cyril Bardsley and the Bishop of Salisbury, tried to convince the Anglican Church to put the Oxford Group movement under its umbrella, but the effort met with failure. Yet Bishop Berggrav of the Norwegian Church claimed that the Oxford Group movement was the most important spiritual movement in Norway since the Reformation.
8. Cursillo is a renewal movement that began in the Roman Catholic Church on the Spanish island of Majorca in the 1940s and later spread to the Episcopal Church. It is a weekend short course in Christianity followed by meetings in small groups. Its participants hold each other accountable in personal piety, study, and Christian action.
9. Robert Thomsen, *Bill W.* (New York: Harper & Row, 1975), 232–33.
10. Walter Clark, *The Oxford Group: Its History and Significance* (Baltimore: Bookman Associates, 1951), 28.
11. Hadley Cantril, *The Psychology of Social Movements* (Melbourne, Fla.: Robert Krieger, 1941), 148–51.
12. Ibid., 147–48.

13. Robertson, *Getting Better*, 63.
14. Ibid., 127.
15. Ibid., 126
16. Morton Kelsey, *Psychology, Medicine, and Christian Healing* (New York: Harper & Row, 1988), 323.
17. Evelyn Woodward, "Poets, Prophets, and Pragmatists," in *The Canticle* (Community of St. Francis), March 1990.
18. The Community of Celebration in Aliquippa, Pennsylvania, is an Anglican model. It is known for its Fisherfolk music and ministry.
19. *Building Christian Communities: Strategy for Renewing the Church* (Dallas: National Ultreya Publications, 1972).
20. Frank M., archivist, in a letter dated April 10, 1990.
21. Al-Anon statistics, Al-Anon Family Headquarters, Inc., New York, 1989.

3 / The Twelve Branches

1. The number ten in Hebrew means forming a community or group and two (which added to ten makes twelve) means the joining together for unity.
2. Ethelbert W. Bullinger, *Number in Scripture* (Grand Rapids: Kregel, 1980), 253–55.
3. *Alcoholics Anonymous Comes of Age*, 161.
4. Irving Harris, *The Breeze of the Spirit: Sam Shoemaker and the Story of Faith at Work* (New York: Seabury Press, 1978), 51.
5. Kurtz, *Not-God*, 69; *Alcoholics Anonymous Comes of Age*, 160–61.
6. Alcoholics Anonymous literature.
7. *Alcoholics Anonymous Comes of Age*, 161.
8. Lean, *On the Trail of a Comet*, 157.
9. Sam Shoemaker, *The Grapevine*, January 1964.
10. Kurtz, *Not-God*, 70, 275.
11. *Alcoholics Anonymous Comes of Age*, 162.
12. AA literature.
13. See Overcomers Outreach, Inc., 2290 W. Whittier Blvd., Suite A/D, LaHabra, CA 90631, or the National Episcopal Coalition on Alcohol, for the biblical references to match the steps.
14. *Al-Anon Faces Alcoholism*, 1988 edition, 229.
15. Grant R. Schnarr, *Unlocking Your Spiritual Potential — A Twelve Step Approach* (St. Meinrad, Ind.: Abbey Press, 1990), 46.
16. St. Ignatius of Loyola was born in Spain and founded the Society of Jesus in 1548. The Spiritual Exercises, followed by a retreatant under spiritual direction, were designed to provide a new kind of spiritual freedom. During the first week spent in retreat there is an examination of conscience followed by confession and communion. The retreatant is to meditate on his or her sins and the power of those sins, to concentrate on making a statement about those sins, to weigh them, to look at "who I am," to consider who God is, and to proclaim the wonders of

God. This is repeated and then summarized. Next the retreatant is to meditate on Hell, with all of his or her imagination and sensory perceptions. During the second week of retreat, the retreatant is to contemplate Christ the King, the Incarnation, and the Nativity with all of his or her senses. The third week is for contemplation on the Last Supper and the Garden of Gethsemane. The fourth week is spent considering how Christ appeared to Mary, the Mother of Jesus, contemplating how to gain love and learning methods of praying. Today retreats are usually one-day or weekend affairs; one might meditate in silence or contemplate the Stations of the Cross.

17. David L. Fleming, *The Spiritual Exercises of St. Ignatius: A Literal Translation and a Contemporary Reading*, ed. George E. Ganss, Study Aids on Jesuit Topics, ser. no. 7 (St. Louis: Institute of Jesuit Studies, 1978), 103.

18. Morton T. Kelsey *Psychology, Medicine and Christian Healing* (New York: Harper & Row, 1988), 243.

19. Written for AA.

20. *Twenty Four Hours a Day* (Center City, Minn.: Hazelden, 1975), thought for January 20.

21. See Robert Forman and Michael Fassino's study at Alvernia College, published in the November 1987 edition of *Addictionary*.

22. Hazelden Educational Materials prints a series of pamphlets, one on each step.

23. Abraham Twerski, *Waking Up Just in Time* (New York: Pharos Books, 1990), 29.

24. M. Scott Peck, M.D., *People of the Lie: The Hope for Healing Human Evil* (New York: Simon & Schuster, 1983).

25. See Patrick J. Carnes, *A Gentle Path through the Twelve Steps* (Irvine, Calif.: CompCare Publishers, 1989).

26. See the Episcopal *Book of Common Prayer* for one form of this confession.

27. Adapted from a chart appearing in Friends in Recovery, *The Twelve Steps: A Spiritual Journey* (San Diego: Recovery Publications, 1988), 109; see also Joan L. Rocosalvo, C.S.J., *The Daily Examen* (University of Scranton).

28. See Ernest Kurtz, *Shame and Guilt: Characteristics of the Dependency Cycle* (Center City, Minn.: Hazelden, 1981). *False shame* is essentially undeserved blame placed on us by others and often leads to scrupulosity. *Real guilt* is when we have caused others harm through what we have said or how we have said things or by what we have done or not done.

29. Abraham Twerski, M.D., Postscript, *Waking Up Just in Time* (New York: Pharos Books, 1990).

30. See *Wellness Letter* (University of California, Berkeley), June 1990, for a discussion of whether there is such a thing as an "addictive personality." Their conclusion is that personality can work for you, not against you, and that no one is chemically, genetically, or psychologically doomed.

31. Dr. Timmen L. Cermak, *A Time to Heal: The Road to Recovery for Adult Children of Alcoholics* (Los Angeles: J. P. Tarcher, 1987), 223, defines co-dependency as follows: (1) continued investment of self-esteem in the ability to control both

oneself and others in the face of serious consequences; (2) assumption of responsibility for meeting other's needs to the exclusion of acknowledging one's own; (3) anxiety and boundary distortions around intimacy and separation; (4) enmeshment in relationships with personality disordered, chemically dependent, other co-dependent and/or impulse disordered individuals; (5) three or more of the following: (a) excessive reliance on denial; (b) constriction of emotions (with or without dramatic outbursts); (c) depression; (d) hypervigilance; (e) compulsions; (f) anxiety; (g) substance abuse; (h) has been the victim of recurrent physical or sexual abuse; (i) stress-related medical illnesses; (j) has remained in a primary relationship with an active substance abuser for at least two years without seeking outside help. See also Pia Mellody with Andrea Wells Miller and J. Keith Miller, *Facing CoDependency* (New York: HarperCollins Publishers, 1989), 210.

4 / The Leaves, the Buds, and the Fruit

1. *Alcoholics Anonymous* (New York: Alcoholics Anonymous World Services, Inc., 1988); Al-Anon has its version, entitled *Al-Anon Faces Alcoholism* (New York: Al-Anon Family Group Headquarters, Inc., 1988).
2. *Alcoholics Anonymous*, xii.
3. Ernest Kurtz, *Not-God*, 186.
4. *Alcoholics Anonymous*, 495–507.

5 / Nourishment

1. Harold S. Kushner, *Who Needs God?* (New York: Summit Books, Simon & Schuster, 1989), 127.
2. See M. Scott Peck, *What Return Can I Make? The Dimensions of the Christian Experience* (New York: Simon & Schuster, 1985).
3. *Twelve Steps and Twelve Traditions* (New York: Al-Anon Family Group Headquarters, Inc., 1986), 22.
4. J. David Else, *Sharing*, newsletter of the Center for Spirituality in Twelve-Step Recovery (99 S. 22nd Street, Pittsburgh, PA 15203).
5. See the results of the Harvard School of Public Health and Boston University research study as reported in the *Wall Street Journal* (September 12, 1991). Of those treated in an in-patient treatment program, 44 percent stayed sober for two years vs. 20 percent who went to AA only.
6. Author's revision of a prayer of confession found in the Episcopal *Book of Common Prayer*.
7. Attributed to Amy Johnstone Flink.

6 / Threats

1. Interview, June 1990.

2. Paul C. Conley and Andrew A. Sorensen, *The Staggering Steeple* (Nashville: Abingdon Press, 1982). 16–132.

3. Ibid., 125.

4. The Interfaith Network in its spring 1990 meeting reported on progress in developing denominational policies toward alcoholism. The General Assembly of the Presbyterian Church has the most comprehensive policy statement. It says that "responsible and non-problematic use of alcohol has been part of human experience and the Judeo-Christian heritage since the beginning of recorded history." It "encourages and supports personal decision to abstain from alcohol" and "urges moderate and responsible use." It also states that "alcohol should not be purchased at church expenses except when authorized by a governing body for use in the Lord's Supper" and that "whenever wine is used in the Lord's Supper, a clearly identifiable nonalcoholic alternative should be available."

5. Distilled liquors were to be distinguished from fermented liquors, such as wine, beer, and ale, which were acceptable because they were naturally fermented.

6. Conley and Sorensen, *The Staggering Steeple,* 119.

7. "New Slavery, New Freedom: A Pastoral Message on Substance Abuse," November 13, 1990.

8. See "Episcopal Lifelines" supplement to *Episcopal Life,* September 1990. The new Coalition president sees about 20 percent of the church nationally being affected by the disease of alcoholism.

9. See Gerald May, *Addiction and Grace* (New York: Harper & Row, 1988), and Keith Miller, *Sin, Overcoming the Ultimate Addiction* (New York: Harper & Row, 1987).

10. Donald Capps, *Life Cycle Theory and Pastoral Care* (Philadelphia: Fortress, 1983), 38. See also Billy Graham, *The Seven Deadly Sins* (Grand Rapids: Zondervan, 1955).

11. Abraham Twerski, *Addictive Thinking* (San Francisco: Harper/Hazelden, 1990), chap. 1.

12. Philip Parham, *Letting God* (New York: Harper & Row, 1987), January 17.

13. See Conley and Sorensen, *The Staggering Steeple,* 112–13, and Howard J. Clinebell, *Understanding and Counseling the Alcoholic* (Nashville: Abingdon, 1982), 104–18, who compares the Salvation Army Rescue Mission solutions, to Emmanuel's approach and Alcoholics Anonymous.

14. Kathleen Fitzgerald, in her book *Alcoholism, the Genetic Inheritance* (Garden City, N.Y.: Doubleday, 1988), describes the blood levels of acetaldehyde, a normal by-product of alcohol metabolism, as well as tetrahydroisquinoline (a heroin-like substance). Brain cell membranes in alcoholics have an unusual amount of thickening; when deprived of alcohol, they work with great discomfort. Current research indicates that women are at greater risk than

men for becoming alcoholics at midlife because they lose the enzyme alcohol dehydrogenase, which breaks down alcohol in the digestive system.

15. *The Church Army News* 4, no. 2 (June 1990).

16. Philip Parham, *Letting God,* March 10.

17. Robert Godley, "Some Theological Reflections on Alcoholism/Chemical Dependency," an unpublished paper.

18. John Baudhuin, "Spirituality and Recovery," 1982, an unpublished paper.

19. Vernon Johnson, in an article entitled "The Divine Commission and Alcoholism," *Saint Luke's Journal of Theology* 21, no. 4 (September 1978), describes a clergy intervention process. As a pastor, he claims, a clergyperson has a license to take the initiative to contact family members who are affected by someone's addiction and to facilitate the intervention process. Data collection, rehearsals with the family, and treatment planning are all part of the process. It is important for clergy to call in a trained intervention specialist if they have no such training.

20. Jacquelyn Small, "A Spiritual Emergence and Addiction: A Transpersonal Approach to Alcoholism and Drug Counseling," *Revision* 10, no. 2 (Fall 1987), 27. She is the director of Eupsychia, Inc., in Austin, Texas, and serves on the faculty of the Institute of Transpersonal Psychology. Her theory is further explained in her book *Transformers: The Therapists of the Future* (Marina del Rey, Calif.: DeVorss, 1982).

21. *Alcoholics Anonymous,* 248.

22. Ibid., 192, 259, 303.

23. I use the personal pronoun "he" or "him" for God because I believe that God has all the attributes of what our human fathers ought to be. But it is difficult for some persons in twelve-step programs to call God "Father" because their childhoods were poisoned by unloving or alcoholic fathers who rejected, abused, or abandoned them. If they choose to call God "she" I am convinced that God him- or herself doesn't mind as long as they can experience God's personal parental love.

24. See Marilyn Ferguson, *The Aquarian Conspiracy: Personal and Social Transformation in the 1980s,* rev. ed. (Los Angeles: J. P. Tarcher, 1981).

25. John Naisbitt and Patricia Aburdene, *Megatrends 2000* (New York: William Morrow, 1987), 280.

26. Ronald Enroth, *Lure of the Cults* (Downers Grove, Ill.: Intervarsity Press, 1987.

27. Naisbitt and Aburdene, *Megatrends 2000,* 282.

28. John A. T. Robinson was the suffragan bishop of Woolrich, 1959–69, in the Church of England. He is the author of *Honest to God.*

29. Katy Butler, "Spirituality Reconsidered," *Networker* (September–October 1990): 35–36.

30. Note Bradshaw's comments in *Healing the Shame That Binds You* (Deerfield Beach, Fla.: Health Communications, 1988).

31. Robert Bellah et al., *Habits of the Heart* (Berkeley: University of California Press, 1985), 245.

32. Morton T. Kelsey, *Psychology, Medicine and Christian Healing* (New York: Harper & Row, 1988), 190.

33. The organization's headquarters is 53 Larch St., Manchester, NH 03102; (603) 668-1876. Albert LaChance is the author of *Greenspirit*.

34. "Twelve Steps for Women Alcoholics," from *Christian Century* (December 6, 1989): 1150–52.

35. Joe Klaas, *The Twelve Steps to Happiness* (Center City, Minn.: Hazelden, 1979).

36. Ernest Kurtz, *Not God*, 23.

37. As described by Ken Ramsey, Director of Gateway Rehabilitation Center in Aliquippa, Pennsylvania, on April 10, 1991.

38. Today we understand more about the biological effects of addiction on addicts who are dually addicted to drugs and alcohol. This co-morbidity makes detox and recovery more difficult. Whereas in the early 1900s alcoholism was associated with depression and personality disorders, today alcoholism is associated with cocaine and tranquilizer addiction, phobia disorders, sexual abuse, schizophrenia, narcissism, and organic brain damage.

39. Gerald May, *Addiction and Grace* (New York: Harper & Row, 1988), 133, 139.

7 / To the Ends of the Earth

1. "Narcology" is the Soviet term that refers to medical treatment hospitals for alcoholics.

2. *Sobriety News*, July/August 1990.

3. *Time*, April 10, 1989.

4. Telephone interview, December 15, 1989. According to Jeffrey Laign, managing editor of the *U.S. Journal of Drug and Alcohol Dependence*, the first meeting was in 1986 ("Soviet Union Faces Addiction Crisis," *U.S. Journal of Drug and Alcohol Dependence* 15, no. 10 [October 1991]).

5. Telephone interview, December 15, 1989.

6. The other drugs prevalent in the U.S.S.R. are barbiturates and hashish.

7. *Sobriety News*, July/August 1990, 6.

8. Interview, March 30, 1991.

9. Interview, March 28, 1991.

10. *Sobriety News*, Winter/Spring 1989, 1, 2.

11. The names are fictitious.

12. *Sobriety News*, Winter/Spring, 1989, 3.

13. Zedaker, *Sobriety News*, August 1990.

14. Telephone interview with Sara P., Alcoholics Anonymous World Service Center.

15. Interview, October 1989.

16. Personal interview.

17. Pittsburgh, November 2, 1989.

18. Telephone interviews, 1989, 1991.

19. Jeffrey Laign, "Soviet Union Faces Addiction Crisis," 10–11. Salus International received funding from Louis Bantel for the training of the staff. $400 will support one Soviet alcoholic in treatment for twenty-eight days. Their address is c/o Mary Kay Wright-Mahler, 56 Elgavilan, Orinda, CA 94563.

20. Ibid.

21. The Russian Orthodox Church recently held its Millennium celebration in Moscow. One Orthodox patriarch described the event as a mighty in-flowing of the Holy Spirit, much like the original Pentecost. It was about that time that the Iron Curtain began to disappear. Now Christians and Jews alike can openly worship, maintain places of worship, and operate schools of religious education. Their Eastern Orthodox liturgy is rich with symbolism, music, art, and light. Poor but alive, both evangelical and orthodox Christianity have managed to survive under persecution.

22. Charles Leerhsen et al., "Unite and Conquer," *Newsweek*, February 5, 1990, 54.

23. A ten-year study by researchers at Stanford University showed that terminally ill cancer patients who participated in weekly support group meetings lived twice as long as others.

24. "The Codependent Cinderella Who Loves Too Much... Fights Back," *Family Networker* (July/August 1990): 55.

25. "Chances Are You're Codependent Too," *New York Times Book Review*, February 11, 1990.

26. "Al-Anon: Then and Now, a Brief History," Al-Anon Family Group Headquarters, Inc., 1986.

27. Preamble, Al-Anon Family Headquarters, Inc., New York, 1983.

28. Defined with the help of Dr. Robert Custer.

29. Henry R. Lesieur, *Understanding Compulsive Gambling* (Center City, Minn.: Hazelden, 1986), 3.

30. From the Tri-State Regional Meeting list, Pittsburgh.

31. *Narcotics Anonymous*, Narcotics Anonymous World Service Office, Van Nuys, Calif., xi.

32. Preamble to OA literature, Overeaters Anonymous, Torrance, Calif.

33. The sugar addiction theory is a minority opinion in the scientific literature. See E. M. Abrahamson, M.D. and A. W. Pezet, M.D., *Body, Mind and Sugar* (New York: Holt & Co., 1951) and Janice K. Phelps, M.D., and Alan E. Nourse, M.D., *The Hidden Addiction and How to Get Free* (Boston: Little Brown, 1986).

34. From SLAA literature, Sex and Love Addicts Anonymous, Boston.

8 / The Church and the "A" Groups: Mutual Challenge

1. Interview, October 5, 1990.

2. Clay Oglesby, "Here I Stand," *United Methodist Reporter*, December 30, 1988.

3. Robert Bellah, et al., *Habits of the Heart,* 246.
4. From Preamble to Overcomers Outreach, Whittier, Calif., 8.
5. F.R.E.E.D.:
Fellowship in Recovery
Reconciliation to God and His Family
Education about Chemicals and Addiction
Edification through Faith in Christ
Dedicated Service to Others
6. "What the Church Has to Learn from Alcoholics Anonymous," The Maryland Diocesan Commission on Alcoholism.
7. Ibid.
8. Barfoot, "Being Blessed or a Blessing," 6.
9. As reported in the *United Methodist Reporter*. These steps were authored by Dr. Vernon J. Bittner and are expanded upon in his books, *You Can Help with Your Healing, Breaking Free,* and *Twelve Steps for Christian Living.* More information on the Twelve Steps for Christian Living can be obtained through the Institute for Christian Living, P.O. Box 22408, Minneapolis MN 55422.

SELECTED TWELVE-STEP BIBLIOGRAPHY

Bittner, Vernon J. *Twelve Steps for Christian Living.* Minneapolis: Institute for Christian Living, 1988.

Carnes, Patrick J. *A Gentle Path through the Twelve Steps.* Irvine, Calif.: CompCare Publishers, 1989.

Friends in Recovery. *The Twelve Steps — A Spiritual Journey.* San Diego: Recovery Publications, 1988.

Friends in Recovery. *The Twelve Steps for Christians.* San Diego: Recovery Publications, 1988.

Grateful Members. *The Twelve Steps for Everyone.* Irvine, Calif.: CompCare Publications, 1977.

Hazelden Foundation. *The Little Red Book.* Center City, Minn.: Harper/Hazelden, 1987.

Hazelden Foundation. Pamphlets on the Twelve Steps. Center City, Minn.: Hazelden Educational Materials, 1982.

Keller, Ron. *The Twelve Steps and Beyond.* Burnsville, Minn.: Prince of Peace Publishing Co., 1989.

Miller, Keith, with Andrea Miller and Pia Mellody. *Hunger for Healing.* New York: Harper & Row, 1991.

Rogers, Ronald L. *The Twelve Steps Revisited.* New York: Bantam Books, 1990.

Schnarr, Grant. *Unlocking Your Spiritual Potential: A Twelve Step Approach.* St. Meinrad, Ind.: Abbey Press, 1990.

Shoemaker, Samuel M., D.D. "Those Twelve Steps, As I Understand Them." *The Grapevine,* January 1964.

Turning to God: Finding a Spiritual Path to Recovery. New York: American Bible Society, 1976.

The Twelve Steps and Twelve Traditions. New York: Al-Anon Family Groups, Inc., 1965.

Twerski, Abraham J., M.D. *Waking Up Just in Time.* New York: Pharos Books, 1990.